WHY DO COPS EAT DONUTS?

JASON KNICKERBOCKER

Why Do Cops Eat Donuts?

Copyright © 2024 by Tax Scout LLC and Jason Knickerbocker

All rights reserved.

To my wife Amy and our kids

Colton, Savannah, Payson and Riley

Love you!

CONTENTS

A Preface | vii
About the Author | xi

50 QUESTIONS

1. So, why do cops eat donuts? | 3
2. Can police officers shoot someone who is running away? | 5
3. How do I get out of a traffic ticket? | 7
4. What is the difference between a police officer, deputy sheriff, state trooper, federal agent, park ranger, and highway patrolman? | 9
5. What is all that stuff police officers wear on their waist and how is it used? | 13
6. What are the different ranks of police officers and what do they do? | 17
7. Why do police officers shoot their gun so many times, or shoot people in the back? | 21
8. What is pepper spray and how does it work? | 23
9. How does a TASER work? | 25
10. What is the difference between a misdemeanor and a felony? | 27
11. What is bail and how does it work? | 29
12. What is the P.I.T. maneuver? | 33
13. Do police officers have to read an arrestee their Miranda rights? | 35
14. Why do police officers carry a gun off duty? | 37
15. How does a radar gun work? | 39
16. What is the police academy like? | 41
17. What are some of the assignments a police officer can work? | 45
18. Do police officers have to pass a physical fitness test? | 47
19. What type of training do police officers get when they are done with the academy? | 49
20. How do you get to fly the police helicopter? | 51
21. How does a police officer become a detective? | 53
22. How does a police officer get onto the SWAT team? | 55
23. How often do police officers practice shooting? | 57

24. What is the minimum or maximum age to become a
    police officer?   59
25. Can you be arrested for being drunk in public?   61
26. Can a police officer commandeer my vehicle?   63
27. Why do so many law enforcement officers complain
    about their leadership?   65
28. Will a police officer shake my hand?   67
29. Why do police officers break up parties?   69
30. Can a police officer leave their jurisdiction during a
    pursuit?   71
31. Can a police officer carry a gun on a plane?   73
32. What is entrapment?   75
33. Are police cars really that fast?   77
34. When can a police officer drive with their lights and
    sirens on?   79
35. Do all police officers wear bullet proof vests?   81
36. When can a police officer force their way into a home?   83
37. Are police officers allowed to use discretion when
    enforcing the law?   85
38. Why do police officers chase a suspect in a car for hours
    instead of just ramming it to end the pursuit?   89
39. How do I get out of a DUI if I am pulled over?   91
40. Can police officers fire a warning shot?   93
41. Can police officers punch someone?   95
42. What should I do if I get pulled over to help make the
    stop as safe as possible?   97
43. Can I shoot someone who breaks into my home?   99
44. Why do police cars have AR-15's in them?   103
45. Do police officers racially profile?   105
46. Why do I get pulled over so much?   107
47. Do police officers have a quota?   109
48. Can a police officer shoot an unarmed suspect?   111
49. Why do cops shoot suspects in the chest instead of
    aiming for the leg?   113
50. If police officers are the good guys, then why are there so
    many bad police shootings?   115

A PREFACE

– GEORGE ORWELL

In late 2022, I retired from being a cop and moved to Arizona from California. My wife and I have been blessed with four wonderful young kids who we both love a lot. As anyone with kids knows, it can be a struggle to get them into bed at night. On top of the regular bed time struggles, we live in a pretty rural area, so at night, it can sometimes be dark and scary. When we are tucking our kids into bed, sometimes they pull the "I'm scared line." After we have tried all the "normal" stuff like saying prayers, turning on a night light, or putting on a relaxing song, I try something unique to my life experiences. I remind my kids that as they are going to bed, there are tough cops, or in our case, deputies driving around looking for bad guys. I remind my kids these men and women will be up all-night driving around ready to protect them at a moment's notice. I tell my kids that the deputies have hundreds of tough friends who will join in any fight and that no bad guy stands a chance against this army of guardians.

This part will make most liberals cry and most child psychologists roll their eyes, but I even tell my kids that from time to time, cops get to "kick the bad guy's ass." We say prayers for the deputies and even for the "bad guys." I remind my kids that usually, the "bad guys" are someone who is suffering through addiction, a terrible childhood or mental health issues, and they need prayers too. However, I make sure to tell my kids that when push comes to shove, we always want the good guys to win regardless of what happens to the bad guy.

In this book, I'll answer 50 questions that I have been asked during my 21-year career. I am writing this book because I have always had a deep love and respect for police officers. Not just because I got to do it for a living, or because police keep me and my family safe but because I really do love law enforcement officers. I want to do what I can to be a voice for them everywhere. I hope to take away some of the mystery of who they are and what they do, because if the public can better understand why cops act the way that they do—then perhaps they'll be more supportive of them.

I admit cops, including me when I was still one, sometimes do some goofy things. Usually, there is a good reason behind it but other times we just mess up. They make mistakes and I made plenty of mistakes myself. However, considering the things they do every day, cops do an exceptional job under difficult circumstances.

If you are reading this book, you are probably interested in law enforcement for one reason or another. You might be related to a cop, you might want to be a cop, you might hate the police or you might find the profession fascinating. Either way, I hope to positively influence someone, somewhere, who ends up interacting with law enforcement.

I want to give a fair warning that I have chosen to leave lots of questions out such as, "How can I get away with robbing a bank?" I do have some pretty good ideas on how you could get away with robbery, but for the sake of humanity, I'm going to keep those to myself. My overall goal for this book is to shed light on what cops do and why they do it, not to help you supplement your retirement by robbing a bank.

The list of questions and answers is compiled from questions strangers asked me when I was in uniform, questions I have answered at community town hall meetings, and even things my extended family has asked me when we drink together.

Throughout this book, I will refer to the generic term of "police officer" or "cop," as this can mean deputy sheriff, state trooper, constable, park ranger, and so on.

ABOUT THE AUTHOR

I am going to step way outside my comfort zone and tell you a little about myself. Most cops, including myself, don't like to talk about ourselves in public. I need to though, so when I answer a question in the book, you can see I'm not talking out of my ass like some "law enforcement experts." Or, maybe you will decide I am talking out of my ass but either way it's good to know who is doing the talking.

One of my first memories was wanting to be a cop. In fact, my family makes fun of me because when I was a small kid, I use to have a plastic badge and a cap gun and would go around pretending I was, "The Sheriff." Fast forward to June of 2000, at the age of 22, I was hired as a deputy sheriff for the Pima County Sheriff's Department in Tucson, Arizona. I went to a 16-week police academy in Tucson and then worked on patrol for almost two years in the Tucson area.

After a few years in Tucson, I decided to relocate to southern California. I wanted to continue being a police officer, so I applied for the Torrance Police Department, the Santa Monica Police Department and the Manhattan Beach Police Department. Manhattan Beach PD was the first department to offer me a job, so I jumped right on it. To my disappointment, I was required to go to the police academy again because it had to be a California POST approved police academy.

The academy Manhattan Beach PD used at the time was the Orange County Sheriff Department's in Orange County, California. This training was a 26-week academy, which was ten weeks longer than the Arizona academy I went to, and to me it was much harder. The Orange County Sheriff's Academy has always prided itself on being one of the hardest academies in the country, both physically and academically.

With some hard work and a lot of luck, I graduated from the Orange County Sheriff's Academy and began field training with Manhattan Beach PD.

From my first day at the academy in Arizona, until my last day on the job in October of 2022, I was blessed to work on a ton of fun assignments. The majority of my time was spent on patrol, which—to me—was the most fun and best way to learn. I also had the opportunity to work as a field training officer, detective and motorcycle officer. My department was small, so we had collateral assignments, which were assignments you do on a part-time basis in addition to your primary assignment. As a collateral duty, I served as a firearms instructor, honor guard member, SWAT team member and hostage negotiator. During my career, I even had the opportunity to become a detective, patrol sergeant, SWAT team commander and a lieutenant.

Since the police department I worked for was not very big, we would use outside agencies to train in various subjects and tactics. I went to the Los Angeles County Sheriff's Department Basic SWAT school, the FBI hostage negotiation school and some other large agencies for firearms, driving, motorcycle, field training and investigations.

Even though I had the opportunity to go to some of the best law enforcement training classes, I am not as experienced or talented as a cop in a big city. (In fact, there are a lot of cops who make me look like a girl scout.) However, even in my short career, because of where Manhattan Beach is located and the cities it is surrounded by, I have seen more than I ever imagined I would.

I have been punched, kicked, spat on, bled on, vomited on, yelled at, attacked, called names and hung up on; I stuck my finger with a dirty drug needle, was bitten by a pit-bull and investigated by internal affairs; I woke up parents at night to tell them their child is dead; I helped drug addicts get their lives together just to see them get back on drugs and die; I saw the bloody guts of plenty of people, and even brains on one too many occasions; I kicked in doors for emergencies or when a "suspicious odor" was coming from a house only to find a rotting corpse inside; and I witnessed little kids treated badly by parents, and elderly parents treated badly by their adult kids.

I had good friends who were cops fired for making one bad decision. I also saw a few cops never get fired even though they should have been. Not because they were bad people but because they could not actually do the job. I lost cops in neighboring cities I barely knew, co-workers, buddies and even friends to fatal car accidents, fatal on-duty and off duty motorcycle accidents, job related cancers, alcohol, drugs and even suicide.

I have chased and tackled a decent number of bad guys and have been in plenty of vehicle pursuits. I have rammed cars, used the PIT maneuver on cars, successfully laid out spike strips and unsuccessfully laid out spike strips. I have been in a handful of physical fights at work and have been injured a time or two, but thankfully not too badly. I shot suspects with my TASER, beanbag shotgun, pepper spray and a 40mm but never with a gun.

I have been on more high-risk search warrants than I can remember in more cities than I can remember as both the primary and supporting agency. I have participated in several negotiations when it worked, as well as when it didn't work, and someone ended up dead. I never got to be the person doing the negotiating, but I acted as support or was the supervisor.

I have been covered in blood from victims and suspects and I mean covered. I have been to officer involved in shootings where officers have won gun fights, tied gun fights and even a few where they lost gunfights.

I laid down my police motorcycle a few times but never crashed it. I even ran over my own foot once when turning on my motorcycle to go after a speeding motorist. It hurt a lot but more importantly for a thin-skinned cop, it was embarrassing! Also, FYI, the speeding motorist got away.

Despite what TV and the news may have you think, I have never lied on the stand or at work. I am an imperfect human. I have lied to friends and family and am no angel, but at work, I really can't remember a time where I lied. Well, I did lie to suspects when it was appropriate like during a sting or interview but never under oath or when I was not supposed to.

I started the job as a sensitive kid raised by a single mom and have been hardened by the last 21 years. I am fortunate to have a happy and optimistic approach to life, but I have had my internal struggles over the last 21 years. I wrestled with anger, jealousy, rage, burnout, frustration and even alcohol a time or two. I probably never would have lasted in a big city, so I am thankful I was hired where I was hired. I think about the fact more cops kill themselves every year than are killed in the line of duty, and I'm grateful to not be in either of those categories.

Embarrassingly enough, I learned through marriage counseling that I have PTSD and was later officially diagnosed with it by a department hired psychologist. I hate to use the term PTSD because it's the cool thing to do these days but it is what it is. However, I share it because I was also told by several psychologists that pretty much any cop with about 10 years on the job has PTSD whether officially diagnosed or not. Please keep this in mind for any cop you are close to and perhaps encourage them to get help if they seem crankier than usual.

By leaning on God, going to counseling, having a new career and focusing on my wife and kids, I'm starting to be more how I was before I became a cop. In addition to my career as a police officer, in 2010 at the age of 32, I temporarily left my job and joined the Army National Guard where I eventually served for 6 years as an infantry platoon leader. My unit mobilized for a deployment to Afghanistan in 2013, but our deployment was canceled weeks before leaving. I was disappointed I never saw combat, but now I am old enough to know to be careful what you wish for.

It is hard to walk away from law enforcement. I could have or maybe even should have stayed on a bit longer, but emotionally it was time for me to go when I did. I am writing this book as a small gesture to those who are still doing the job that gets harder and harder every day.

As I am finishing this book, I am thinking of Officer Chad Swanson. I trained Chad for 4 weeks as one of his FTOs and then worked with him for about 10 years, including time as his co-worker, supervisor and teammate on the SWAT team. I would not claim to be friends, but we were cordial at work, had a few drinks off duty together at various events and even played craps in Las Vegas together once. On October 4, 2023, Chad was killed in an on-duty police motorcycle accident. He was a father to three young boys, a husband and a great cop.

In law enforcement, losing friends or even co-workers hits you really hard because of the comradery and strong bonds you build. Chad died a few years after I retired, but right or wrong, had I still been a cop when he was killed, I don't know if I could have handled it. I went to his funeral and I saw my co-workers and friends in a lot of pain. I also saw his family in pain and saw his three young boys who will unfortunately have to grow up without him in pain. It hurt deep deep down inside me to see it. I love the tight bonds and relationships you build in law enforcement, but they are also a double-edged sword and can make you hurt a lot when something bad happens.

In my experience, almost every rookie cop goes into law enforcement with plenty of energy and optimism, but eventually gets chewed up and spat out about 20 years down the road—if they're so fortunate. For a thin skinned, dorky kid, I had about all I can take, and for that reason, I am now writing about being a cop and not still wearing a badge. This book is my final farewell to law enforcement.

50 QUESTIONS

QUESTION 1
SO, WHY DO COPS EAT DONUTS?

Cops used to eat donuts a lot because it was fast, safe and cheap. It was a place they could hang out past midnight to get out of the cold. All in all, this stigma has stuck, and is hard to shake off.

I think a better way to put it: why are some cops so overweight? I will admit, some of the cops people see during daytime hours are overweight. Most cops working daytime, especially on weekdays, are senior officers. Some of the older cops have let themselves go physically and they are the ones the public see the most.

On weekend nights or graveyard shifts, these cops are generally younger and in better shape. Actually, even the older cops on graveyard are usually in even better shape than the daytime cops. This is because—in general—graveyard cops take their job a little more seriously and really understand the danger of not being prepared physically or mentally.

The truth is, there is such a poor stigma about cops eating donuts that when I was craving a donut, I would not buy one while in uniform. I didn't want to end up on social media looking like a dork. If I was seriously craving a donut, I would call my wife and see if she wanted to meet up and grab coffee behind a retail store. If she said yes, then I would (of course) ask her to grab me a donut or two on the way!

QUESTION 2
CAN POLICE OFFICERS SHOOT SOMEONE WHO IS RUNNING AWAY?

The answer to this question is a complicated yes. When a police officer is justified in using lethal force, they can use any force necessary to stop the suspect. This means if the suspect does something that warrants the use of deadly force and then runs away, the cop can shoot him/ her in the back. To some, this may seem "unjust" but if you consider the violent nature of the encounter, it makes sense.

Police officers are not bound by code of some western movie's justice. They are instead bound by a duty and oath to protect the innocent. If a suspect robs a bank, shoots the teller and flees the scene, the responding officers can shoot him/her in the back and be completely justified in doing so. The reason police officers can shoot a suspect in the back is because the suspect has shown a propensity for violence and poses too much of a threat to risk letting them escape where they can kill again. What if your family member was grabbing a coffee across the street and the escaped robber was running towards them? Would you want the police to allow him to get inside or should they stop him by any means possible before he hurts someone else?

That is a very black and white scenario, and as you know, real life can be all shades of gray. For instance, what if the suspect was holding a gun but didn't shoot anyone in the bank they robbed? What if they used a note that said they had a gun, but no one saw the actual gun? What if it was a knife or a baseball bat? What if they fired a couple rounds and the gun jammed, and they dropped it and ran off with nothing in their hands? Is it possible a crook would carry two guns? I would not assume that after a suspect tried to kill someone, they are instantly harmless just because they dropped a gun. There is no "olly olly oxen free" for the suspect after showing they are a danger to society.

There are so many scenarios that can happen, and no matter the outcome, Monday morning quarterbacks will be there. These "experts" will attack and review a police officer's split-second decision from the safety of a computer screen. It is not at all dissimilar to the game of football, where they replay a catch by the receiver over and over from multiple angles in slow motion—the first call is not always right. Let's say the officer's call was not right, should they be jailed for it?

I am obviously biased, but in my experience, the suspect is almost always responsible for what happens and not the police officer.

HOW DO I GET OUT OF A TRAFFIC TICKET?

This is the number one question I got when I was a police officer. I don't mind telling you how, because chances are if you do get pulled over, the police officer already has a pretty good idea on whether they are going to write you a ticket. There may be something you can do to sway the officer one way or another, but chances are your fate has been sealed.

For example, if you get pulled over by a motorcycle officer or a state trooper, chances are you will get a ticket. These officers are hired and put on the road for one purpose and that is to make the road safe. They write tickets to address issues such as speeding or running a stop sign. They believe in the benefits of writing tickets and think they are necessary for the overall safety of our roads. You can ask for a warning, and if the stars are aligned, you may just get one. You can also admit you were speeding and ask if there is a non-moving violation, they can cite you for instead for a moving violation. (This will prevent your insurance rates from going up.)

So, how do you get out of a ticket from the police officer on patrol? If you get pulled over, the officer is either planning on writing you a ticket, giving a warning, or is undecided. No matter the case, if you are honest and polite, then you have a better chance of receiving a warning than if you are rude and arrogant. If you genuinely apologize and politely ask for a warning, then it's likely you'll get one. On the other hand, if you are rude, deny responsibility or somehow piss the police officer off, chances are there will no warning and you may even get a couple of extra citations for things such as no insurance, seatbelt, lighting issues, etc.

I want to be clear about one thing.: Honesty does not guarantee a warning. If you *are* honest and the police officer is set on writing you a ticket, he may take notes of your genuine confession and use the notes in court. Bottom line is—be nice and respectful, ask for a warning and hope for the best.

On a side note, when I was in college, I got a few tickets of my own. I fought them, and because the officer did not show up to court, my tickets were dismissed. Make no mistake, I was guilty. My plan for court was to explain I was in the wrong and to humbly ask the judge to consider reducing the fine or making it a non-moving violation.

As an adult, I got pulled over about three times, and after the officers found out I was a cop, they let me go with a warning. I also got one red light camera ticket as a cop, and I paid the fine because I was guilty. So, no, even cops do not get away with some traffic violations.

QUESTION 4

WHAT IS THE DIFFERENCE BETWEEN A POLICE OFFICER, DEPUTY SHERIFF, STATE TROOPER, FEDERAL AGENT, PARK RANGER, AND HIGHWAY PATROLMAN?

The titles and names are all from various types of peace officers. They all have different jurisdictions, responsibilities and functions. However, they also have a lot in common as well.

The oldest form of law enforcement is the sheriff. It is a term derived from the early 1300's when the Englishmen first coined the title "Shire Reeve." The Shire Reeve was the principal person responsible for keeping peace in the shire. In the United States, there is one sheriff per county and he or she supervises the deputy sheriffs.

The sheriff is responsible for maintaining county jails and providing law enforcement in unincorporated areas of the county. Normally, the sheriff's department will also be responsible for search and rescue operations. They have the same powers of arrest as any peace officer. They generally cover a larger geographic area than a police department due to the fact that cities are smaller than most counties.

According to Wikipedia, in the United States, there are 3,141 counties. The largest county geographically is San Bernardino County in southern California. It is approximately 20,000 square miles and the Sheriff's Department employs approximately 3,400 sworn and non-sworn employees. The highest population of any county is Los

Angeles County in southern California. In 2023, the Los Angeles County Sheriff's Department had approximately 9,915 sheriff's deputies, not counting over 9,244 support staff of dispatchers, secretaries, mechanics, technicians, or scientists.

A police officer is responsible for police functions inside of the city limits. The head of a police department is the police chief. There is only one police chief per police department, but there could be several police chiefs and police departments in one county.

Some police departments may have only one or two police officers. On the other hand, according to Wikipedia, in 2023 the New York Police Department had an operating budget of 6 billion dollars and employed over 40,000 people, including over 30,000 police officers. The NYPD has 77 precincts, 12 transit districts, 9 housing police service areas, 9,624 police cars, 29 police boats, 8 helicopters, 45 horses and 34 dogs.

A state trooper or highway patrol officer patrols highways throughout the United States. Their main focus is traffic enforcement and safety on the highways and freeways. They will also respond to crimes that occur on highways, hit-and-run investigations, serious injuries or fatal traffic accidents and frequently have specialized units such as SWAT teams or undercover narcotics teams. Highway patrol officers and state troopers are employed by their respective states and have jurisdiction throughout that state.

Now that you have a basic understanding of local and state law enforcement, let's dive into federal law enforcement. Some of the larger, well-known federal agencies include the FBI (Federal Bureau of Investigation), ATF (Alcohol Tobacco and Firearms), DEA (Drug Enforcement Agency), CIA (Central Intelligence Agency), the Federal Marshalls Office and the Secret Service. It does not take a rocket scientist to see that for the most part, the job description and duties are listed directly in the title of the respective agency. Something to keep in mind is that just because the ATF may specialize in firearms does not mean the FBI or Marshalls would not investigate and possibly arrest someone for federal firearm violations.

The biggest distinction between federal law enforcement and local law enforcement is that federal agents investigate federal crimes such as terrorism, drug trafficking and other national issues. They also frequently take the lead on cross-state crimes as well as international investigations. For example, the DEA would investigate a drug cartel transporting drugs into the US and a police officer would investigate the drug dealer on the street.

If you or someone you know is considering a career in law enforcement, there are a few things to consider. A career as a police officer or deputy sheriff will require you to live close enough to the city or county you work for to commute. A career at a state agency will allow you to live almost anywhere within the state you're living in, and a career in federal law enforcement will allow and /or require you to live in various locations within the USA or even the world.

WHAT IS ALL THAT STUFF POLICE OFFICERS WEAR ON THEIR WAIST AND HOW IS IT USED?

The belt is usually referred to as a "Duty Belt" or "Sam Brown." The term Sam Brown dates back to British army officers serving in India in the 19th century. A Sam Brown is really a belt with a shoulder strap and most modern law enforcement agencies do not wear the shoulder strap, but they still call it a Sam Brown.

Over the years, more and more tools have been added to the duty belts of police officers. In the early 20th century, police officers would carry a nightstick and a pistol, but these days, they carry much more.

Police officers still carry pistols in holsters and extra ammunition in magazines on their waists. I call them magazines, not "clips" because that is their proper name. Not many police officers still carry revolvers, but if they do, the extra ammunition is in a speed loader.

The belt carries a radio which sometimes has a lapel microphone or earpiece. It also holds a pepper spray can in a round container. A long time ago, police officers would carry mace, but pepper spray was more effective and safer than mace, so it became the norm. Additionally, the belt holds one or two pairs of handcuffs.

Almost all police officers in uniform are required to carry Tasers. These Tasers shoot out a pair of darts with a wire attached and shock the suspect causing pain and loss of muscle control. The public has a false perception in that Tasers are fail proof, and criticized police officers for shooting their gun when instead they could have used the Taser. Tasers can fail to stop a suspect and are not the appropriate tool in certain life and death situations.

Most agencies still carry a baton of some sort and there are three main types of batons. The PR-24 nightstick which has a distinct side handle; A "straight stick", which is exactly what its name describes and is made of wood, aluminum or plastic. An expandable baton or ASP as it is sometimes called. An ASP is a short metal stick like a giant car antenna that can telescope out into a solid hard piece of metal which can be used as a striking weapon.

Police officers often carry a tourniquet as well. Lessons from the wars in Iraq and Afghanistan have been brought back by veterans who served in the military and then became cops. They have introduced the tourniquet and shared its valuable lifesaving ability. These tourniquets have been used hundreds if not thousands of times to save police officers, victims, and are even used to save suspects after they are shot by the police.

When I was a new cop, if you had to shoot a bad guy, then you would get him or her help when you could, but it was not a priority—and if they died, so be it. In all honesty, if someone shoots at a cop, I believe they deserve to face the consequences of their actions. It ultimately saves money, time, and the space in jail. On the contrary, if someone gets shot by a cop mistakenly, or because they are mentally ill then they deserve all the help they can get.

Regardless of my opinion, now days, police officers are expected to turn from warrior to savior when the gunfire stops. Ask yourself if you could do that? If someone tried to kill you and stop you from seeing your wife, your kids, your parents, could you then immediately switch gears and save their life? Or what if they killed your co-worker? Heck,

I get mad when someone cuts me off while driving, or honks at me—never mind if they tried to kill me or my friends.

There is one more item that has been added in the last decade which is a sign of the times. It is the infamous body camera. When I started over twenty years ago, a police officer's word was all that was needed. Now police are expected to capture everything on camera.

Police work can at times be brutal and it is terrible to see a man shot and then bleed to death. Even if they are the "bad guy", having a man's death recorded and played over and over, has not and will not help the image of law enforcement.

Forty years ago, no one imagined a Taser or camera would be on a police belt, so we can only watch to see what the future holds.

WHAT ARE THE DIFFERENT RANKS OF POLICE OFFICERS AND WHAT DO THEY DO?

The beginning rank is typically police officer, deputy sheriff or state trooper, depending on where they work. There is no requirement to be promoted, so this rank can be the rank for an entire officer's career.

The next step after officer, deputy or trooper is to become a field training officer or "FTO." Depending which department you work for, this can mean you are a first line supervisor, or it can mean you are not responsible for supervising anyone except your trainee. FTO is one of the most important jobs for any police officer—period, end of story.

Usually, as an FTO, you supervise only your trainee or "boot" as they are sometimes referred to. However, most FTOs are looked up to by junior officers and junior officers will often go to an FTO for advice. FTOs should have at least 3 to 5 years on the job before they begin training new police officers but spending more time on the job is ideal. Equally as important to time on the job is intelligence, work ethic, leadership abilities, street smarts and common sense.

FTOs will have to go to specialized training for anywhere from 3 to 14 days on average. This training will help them learn basic supervision, how to teach, mentor and advise. It will also teach them how and why to document performance. A paper trail detailing how good or terrible a trainee is performing is very important. If they get lost in the locker room or can't fight their way out of a wet paper bag, it will have to be documented. As with all professions, proper documentation will help protect the department from a wrongful termination lawsuit. The FTO will have their trainee for a limited time, such as 3 to 6 weeks, and then the trainee will go on to a new FTO. Of course, DEI nonsense and weak leadership play a huge part in field training programs but that is another discussion in and of itself.

Some police departments have a position such as a corporal, lead police officer or acting watch commander. Basically, they are the person in charge of the shift or patrol team assigned to a certain area of the city when a sergeant is unavailable, or if the issue does not warrant a sergeant's attention. Depending on where you work and how busy the department is, a corporal usually has at least 3 to 6 years on the job.

The first leadership position that is pretty standard across the United States—and in my experience the most difficult—is sergeant. Sergeants oversee a shift and have the responsibility of running the day-to-day operations.

If you are an officer and you are not sure about something, and time allows, you can call a sergeant to help you decide. In addition to everyday work issues, a good sergeant will take time to help the officers they supervise with everyday things. I have had good sergeants talk with me about family issues, bills, setting up benefits, investing in deferred compensation, getting my gear squared away, and even career-altering decisions like whether to promote.

The next level of supervisor is lieutenant, and they are responsible for supervising sergeants. In a large city there could be 3 different patrol teams working at once. These teams could be composed of 6 officers and 1 sergeant each. The officers and sergeants perform their duties in the city while handling calls, and the lieutenant would be in the station serving as the watch commander. The lieutenant manages notifications of major incidents, approving reports, sergeant evaluations, staffing and equipment requests. A good lieutenant will help make sure the sergeant is caring for and mentoring their team out in the field.

After lieutenant, things can change from agency to agency but at most police agencies, the next rank is captain. A captain would be in charge of a division or bureau, and they forecast what assets will be needed. They manage staffing requirements, crime trends, allocate officers, and manage budgets.

In large agencies such as the LAPD and the Los Angeles Sheriff's Department, a captain is the head person of a patrol area. For example, there is one captain in charge of LAPD Pacific division. He or she is essentially the police chief for that division.

Depending on the agency, city, county or state, there may be ranks after captain. These ranks are commander, major or deputy chief, and depend on the size, command structure and culture of an agency.

The highest rank is chief of police, sheriff, or sometimes director. These people represent the head of law enforcement organizations. The sheriff is elected, the director is appointed, and the chief of police is interviewed and hired. Regardless of the title, they all have similar roles. They are the director and political figurehead of the organization and the person responsible for its accomplishments and failures. Sheriffs and directors enjoy some political freedom and autonomy when they run their organization because they have been elected for a set amount of time, or appointed for a set amount of time.

Police chiefs on the other hand, slowly turn into political puppets, who are at the beck and call of city council members. In the past, police chiefs enjoyed the same civil service protection as police officers, however, today most police chiefs are hired as what is called an "at will position." This means they can be fired at any time without cause. This is very bad for police agencies and has gradually turned police chiefs from leaders to political puppets. So, with this new shift, police chiefs must now focus on not losing their jobs rather than on making good and sound decisions to protect their communities.

It is easy to just complain. However, I do have a possible solution if anyone is listening. I would restore the civil service protection for police chiefs. If they had this protection, they could run their department as they see fit, stand up for their police officers and push back against the liberal mob mentality. Yes, there is always the risk of the bad ones you can't fire—but over time, it would improve police departments. However, as it stands now, you have city council members running departments through a puppet police chief.

WHY DO POLICE OFFICERS SHOOT THEIR GUN SO MANY TIMES, OR SHOOT PEOPLE IN THE BACK?

Unless you shoot a suspect in their brain or spinal column, they will be able to continue to fight until they lose enough blood and go unconscious. If a suspect is shot right through the heart, they can have up to a minute to use whatever weapon they have to wreak havoc. This means when a police officer is shooting a suspect, the suspect is usually still fighting. As the suspect fights back, an officer may think they are missing and continue to fire. If the officer knows they are hitting the suspect, they may not be sure if the shots are going to stop the suspect or even if the suspect is wearing body armor. By the time the suspect stops fighting, they may have been shot many more times than "needed" to actually stop them, but under high intensity circumstances, the officer would have no way of knowing that until the dust settles.

Another reasons officers end up shooting a suspect so many times is perception and reaction time. Without getting into the science behind it, there are perceptions and reaction times that come into play when doing anything physical. If you are playing catch with your kid and they look away before you throw the ball— more times than not, even though the ball is still in your hand, you let it go and accidentally hit your kid.

Similarly, if the suspect points a gun and then drops it and turns to run, the police officer may not have been able to react to the quick change of events, and fired off three shots into the back of the now unarmed suspect. There is no malice intent on the behalf of the police officer, but there is now a dead suspect who has been shot three times in the back after dropping a gun.

Perception and reaction times are affected by everyday life such as sleep, diet, age, physical fitness, training, etc. So, the expectations for police officers to fire the right amount of shots at the perfect time in the correct place is unrealistic. Next time you hear on the news that a police officer shot someone eleven times, including four times in the back, consider perception and reaction.

QUESTION 8
WHAT IS PEPPER SPRAY AND HOW DOES IT WORK?

Pepper spray is a chemical irritant that is literally made from peppers. It replaced MACE years ago and is the standard for law enforcement agencies throughout the United States. It is either worn on duty belts in small bottles or carried in much larger spray cans in jails or at large civil disturbances. The peppers used to make it are refined into a concentrated formula that burns your eyes and mucus membranes. It's kind of like essential oils but instead of relaxing you or helping you sleep; it makes your face feel like it's on fire and that you're going blind! The intensity or quality of the pepper spray is measured in units of heat. The higher the heat rating, the worse it feels to get sprayed with it.

I can tell you from experience that it is very painful and debilitating to be sprayed in the face. At both police academies I attended, I had to be sprayed in the face with my eyes open and then had to function long enough to call for backup, fight back against the instructor then get the suspect into handcuffs. In my opinion, there are several reasons they spray trainees in police academies. They need to show you how debilitating it is so if you are ever sprayed, you know what to expect. They need to teach you that if sprayed, you might have to resort to deadly force to defend yourself. You also need to know how bad it hurts so that you don't go around spraying anyone who puts up the slightest resistance. Finally, I believe or maybe I hope it is a hidden method to test and toughen up police recruits. If you volunteer to stand with your eyes open knowing you're going suffer badly, you come out a little tougher.

I am sure at some agencies, weak leadership has stopped recruits from being sprayed in the face. However, for those who still spray recruits, they know the importance of testing and toughening cops up for the streets.

An interesting side note about pepper spray I witnessed on more than one occasion, is it does not work on everyone. I still remember very clearly there was one guy in my academy in Arizona who was not affected by the spray. He loved spicy food and ate it all the time so we all figured this was the reason it didn't affect him but who knows. Whatever the reason, he only reported being slightly uncomfortable but was otherwise unfazed. I have also experienced a few suspects who were high on drugs or extremely intoxicated not being affected by it at all.

QUESTION 9
HOW DOES A TASER WORK?

I don't work for TASER, nor have I received their permission to write about them. TASER is a brand name for the generic term of a "conductive energy device." I only carried a TASER brand conductive energy device and never used any other brand, or even saw any other brand on the street. There were other brands at police trade shows or sales demonstrations, but it seems TASER is the standard with almost all U.S. law enforcement agencies. In short, TASERS, or conductive energy devices, conduct electricity, but I will give you a better answer than that!

You can deploy a TASER against a suspect in one of two ways. The first way is by shooting two darts from a cartridge on the end of the TASER at the suspect. When the darts hit the suspect, electricity travels from small wires on the TASER to each dart. This completes the circuit from the TASER. Once the TASER hits the suspect, the electricity causes temporary pain and loss of muscle control.

I am not an engineer and don't work for TASER, so take what I say with a grain of salt, but the TASER basically takes control of your muscles. While training in the academy, I experienced about 2 seconds of a TASER, and no matter how hard I tried to wrestle against it, I could not gain control over my own muscles. Remarkably, TASERS are extremely safe and do not affect the heart muscle for reasons unknown to me. In my experience, as soon as the TASER shuts off, you regain all muscle control.

The other way the TASER works is in a "contact tase", otherwise known as a drive stun. You can drive the "barrel" end of the TASER into the suspect and cause localized pain in order to gain compliance. The drive stun does not affect a large muscle group, so it does not take control over your body like being shot with the darts will. However, it is still a very useful tool.

Like many law enforcement tools, a TASER or conductive energy device is not perfect. They don't always work, as TASERS can sometimes be defeated by knowledgeable hardened criminals.

Another issue with the use of TASERS (like all fun things in life) are attorneys. When a TASER is used against someone high on drugs and they die after a long and violent fight with the police, you can be sure a lawsuit will be filed. Forget the fact the suspect snorted enough cocaine and fentanyl to supply Las Vegas for two weeks, let's blame the police and the TASER!

QUESTION 10
WHAT IS THE DIFFERENCE BETWEEN A MISDEMEANOR AND A FELONY?

The difference between a felony and misdemeanor is where a suspect serves their time; the amount of time a suspect can receive and the after effects once the suspect gets released. All states are different, but there are few constants among states when it comes to felonies and misdemeanors.

A misdemeanor is less serious than a felony and is usually punishable by a fine and/or incarceration in a county jail for up to one year. Once a suspect serves their time, there are usually no additional losses of rights or privileges.

A felony is punishable by a fine and/or punishment in a state prison for terms up to life in prison or even the death penalty. In addition to judicial punishment, if the suspect is convicted of a felony, they lose certain privileges such as their right to vote, the right to run for public office or possess a firearm.

A person can get probation for being convicted of a felony or misdemeanor, but only a person convicted of a felony can be placed on parole. Some states have different classes of misdemeanors or felonies as well, but they all fall within the above definitions.

QUESTION 11
WHAT IS BAIL AND HOW DOES IT WORK?

Growing up, when I saw on the news that someone was "bailed out", I always thought that meant they were free. It always bothered me because I thought it meant if you were rich, you could do anything and get away with it. Now that I am all grown up, I unfortunately realized that is kind of true but at least not with bail.

Being bailed out means the suspect paid to be initially released, but they still have to go to court to face their charges.

In most states, crimes have a set bail range. The bail amount is set upon the suspect's arrest or by a judge at their first appearance later in court. For example, if a suspect gets arrested for a felony such as stealing a car, the bail could range between $10,000 and $100,000. The bail amount gets determined within this range based upon several factors. The factors could include the suspect's criminal record, how many cars they stole, if anyone was hurt in the process, and if they fought against the police. Depending on the factors listed, let's say the bail is set at $50,000. These would be your four options:

Option 1: Remain in custody until the court case is adjudicated. Depending on the seriousness of the crime, the complexity of the investigation and the time the suspect needs to prepare a legal defense, this could take months or even years. Meanwhile, the suspect will sit in jail and wait for their day in court. If found guilty, the suspect will get credit for the days they spent in custody and remain in jail for the remainder of their sentence. If the suspect is found innocent, they walk out of the court room as a free man. But the suspect receives no credit, money, or anything from the time they were in jail.

Option 2: Come up with the cash necessary either by having someone get their money out of the bank, or through someone who is able to lend money. This person would have to post the entire amount of $50,000 and leave it with the department that arrested the suspect or at the courthouse they are assigned to. If the suspect chooses this option, they will get all their bail money back, so long as they show up to all their court cases and don't flee. If the defendant misses a court date, they become a wanted person, and the money will be forfeited. This means if their sister emptied their 401k just to post bail for them, she loses the entire amount. If the suspect doesn't flee, they get all the money back regardless if they are found innocent or guilty. To sum up, the money is just a promise to go to all the court dates until the trial is concluded.

Option 3: Hire a bail bondsman. The bail bondsman will review the facts regarding the defendant's arrest and make a risk assessment to see if they are worth posting bail for. If the bail bondsman decides they are willing to risk posting the defendant's bail, they will come up with the entire $50,000. The suspect will then have to give them a fee in which they both agree upon. This is how bail bondsman they make their money, and this is why they are willing to risk losing the money if the suspect misses a court date. The typical going rate for most bondsman is 10% of the full bond amount. This can vary from state to state, or even depending on the flight risk or seriousness of the crime.

If a bondsman posts bail and the suspect doesn't show up to court, this is when the bounty hunter comes looking for them. The bounty hunter is either the person who posted the money or they got hired by the bail bondsman. The bounty hunter gets a reward from the bail bondsman for locating the suspect. Although the bail bondsman has to pay for the suspect to be captured and returned, the price is considerably less than losing the full bail amount.

Option 4: In some cases, for certain crimes, if the suspect has a clean arrest record, they can ask to be released on their own recognizance. Basically, the suspect has to explain what happened to the judge, and the judge can review, reduce, or even cancel the bail. The suspect is then required to go to all the required court dates until their case is completed—just as they would if they had bailed out.

QUESTION 12
WHAT IS THE P.I.T. MANEUVER?

The P.I.T. stands for Pursuit Intervention Technique. It is a slow to medium speed maneuver designed to safely spin a suspect's car out of control by using the police car's front bumper and/or quarter panel to push the suspect's rear bumper (or quarter panel) to the side. Once the suspect's vehicle spins out, other officers then use their vehicles to block the suspect's vehicle and take them into custody.

Some departments will allow the P.I.T. and include it in their policies, and other departments are too afraid or too risk averse to allow officers to use it. The P.I.T. comes with risks, but police work is inherently risky, and to be a good cop there are always risks involved.

Although this may sound shocking, some criminals are bad and they like to fight, run, spit, kick and even flee in cars. Perhaps the most ironic thing about the P.I.T. maneuver is it's actually safer than a prolonged police pursuit. Even with the P.I.T. maneuver's gamble, it's a very useful and very safe maneuver that all departments should be able to use to catch criminals.

QUESTION 13

DO POLICE OFFICERS HAVE TO READ AN ARRESTEE THEIR MIRANDA RIGHTS?

A lot of people think police officers must read Miranda rights to anyone they arrest. Miranda rights are a bit too complicated and important of a subject to dive into for this question. I also don't want to give out too much information (which could help a suspect), but I can tell you Miranda rights only need to be read in certain situations.

Often times, people I arrested—especially when they were drunk—would say to me, "Hey, you didn't read me my rights!" Depending on how long of a shift it had been, I would smile, tell them thanks for reminding me and continue what I was doing without reading their rights. This made them mad, and they would tell me how they were going to sue me and get off without charges. I would just smile again and continue with my duties. I know not answering them was kind of an asshole move, but as a cop, we must have a sense of humor to make it through a career.

Just to further clarify, if the arrestee is friendly, I'm nice to them and will take the time to explain why I didn't have to read them their rights.

QUESTION 14
WHY DO POLICE OFFICERS CARRY A GUN OFF DUTY?

Police officers carry their gun on them in case there is a life and death situation in which they can respond to, such as an active shooter. As a general rule, most of the police officers I know won't intervene for any minor crimes or even a major crime *unless* it is a life and death situation. If no one is in danger, most police officers are instructed to act as great witnesses and gather as much information as they can.

Cops also carry guns just as an insurance policy to keep them safe from people they have arrested in the past. Sometimes criminals may want to seek revenge if they run into the cop who arrested them. There is an interesting story of a suspect confronting former UFC fighter Forrest Griffin. Luckily Forrest can do more than hold his own, but if you research the story, you will see how bad it could have gotten.

When a police officer is off duty, the risk of getting involved tends to outweigh the reward. If a police officer is off duty, they don't have all their tools, ballistic vest or police radio. Another dangerous aspect is they are not in uniform. Since they are in plain clothes, arriving officers or concerned citizens might view them as a threat and could hurt the off-duty officer. Unfortunately, there are lots of incidents when an off-duty cop was shot by responding officers or citizens who thought they were the suspect when then were actually in plain clothes just trying to help.

An expert for using force in off-duty situations is retired US Army Lieutenant Colonel Grossman. He has a saying that "the only thing that will stop a bad guy with a gun is a good guy with a gun." He also said something else that got stuck in my head. He said that if a police officer didn't have their gun on them when they could have stopped a tragedy, they would never forgive themselves. He is right, and since hearing him talk, I have never left my gun at home. A gun is inconvenient, uncomfortable, and takes a lot of mental energy to carry. At times, I wish I had never heard those words come out of Lieutenant Colonel Grossman's mouth, but I did.

QUESTION 15
HOW DOES A RADAR GUN WORK?

There are two primary types of radar guns law enforcement use, Laser and Doppler. Doppler radar guns shoot out a large radar beam that grows as it gets bigger. This beam strikes the largest or most reflective moving object and travels back towards the radar gun. It calculates the time the beam takes to travel back and visually displays the speed on a screen.

These radar guns are very accurate, but if the operator is not properly trained, they can read the speed of a different vehicle than they actually think they are tracking. This happens because although there may be a small sports car going 55 mph, a larger truck next to it may be going 65 mph, and the signal of the larger truck gets displayed on the radar gun. This is where the officer's training and experience comes into play. A well-trained officer will know which vehicle is traveling faster and correctly track the right vehicle.

Mistakes with Dopler radar can happen, but overall, I think officers make very few mistakes when it comes to using the Doppler radar.

The second type of radar is the laser radar, also known as a Lidar. This radar is extremely accurate and easy to use. It can literally be used by a child with no training and is almost impossible to make a mistake with. I would let kids try it on moving cars when I was a motor officer, and they did it perfectly with no training.

Lidar guns work by shooting a small invisible laser at a moving target. When you aim it at a vehicle and pull the trigger, it displays the speed and locks it in, which adds to its accuracy.

You may wonder why not all radar guns are Lidar. It's because Lidar can only be used while the operator is sitting still, and they have to be held in your hand when being used. This means when a state trooper on a single lane highway is driving towards you, they can't use a Lidar to obtain your speed. However, they can use Doppler radar because it shoots out a large beam that bounces off objects and displays your speed. Doppler radar guns mounted in patrol cars can calculate the patrol car's speed and the speed of any vehicle approaching it.

If you are approaching a police officer on a rural road either from the back or front regardless of if they are moving towards or away from you, chances are they are watching how fast you are diving with their Dopler radar.

QUESTION 16
WHAT IS THE POLICE ACADEMY LIKE?

It depends on where you go for the police academy or how that academy is run, but most are extremely physically and mentally demanding. I had no idea when I was hired as a young kid at the age of 22 what it would be like. I was pretty clueless until day one when they started screaming at me and telling me to do pushups. Thankfully, I had grown up watching Commando, Rambo, Full Metal Jacket and Platoon over and over so I actually kind of liked it. Don't get me wrong, I don't want to go to the academy again but at the time as a young man, it was kind of fun.

Police academies are run similar to military boot camps, however most academies allow you to go home at night and on the weekends. They are typically between 12 and 26 weeks long depending on the type of law enforcement and the specific state requirements.

Although academies throughout the country are different, they all have one purpose in mind: They need to change an ordinary civilian who might never have been yelled at, or in a fight into a disciplined, thick skinned, tactically sound, physically and mentally tough rookie cop.

Most police officers today are more skilled and trained than any police officer the world has ever seen. With technology, media scrutiny, ever-changing laws and ambulance chasing attorneys, a police officer truly needs to be a jack-of-all-trades. They might need to stand with their mouths shut and listen patiently to a drunk yuppie calling them a "pig" without knocking them out cold. Then they may have to jump into their patrol car, drive as fast as they can to a home invasion robbery and physically beat a parolee who is hell bent on never going back to prison into submission. After they finish their report and get a chance to eat a quick snack, they may respond to a report of identity theft, which is a complicated matter to investigate and takes computer skills, analytical skills and most of all a lot of common sense. They need to handle all of these situations while regular life is running full speed ahead in the background.

In order for police officers to be prepared for an ever-changing, difficult and dangerous job, they are taught various things in the academy. They are taught report writing; computer skills; how to wear their uniform; how to carry and use their equipment; how to drive fast; first aid; how to fight, how to shoot; how to maintain their composure under stress; how to respond to various 9-1-1 calls; and how to be confident or at least look confident.

The beginning of the academy is used to weed out the recruits who don't really want to be there. If you manage to not quit, not get fired or physically injured during the first few months of the academy, recruits will start to learn the fun stuff.

One of the more interesting things in the academy I had no idea about was called the "will to survive" fight. I am pretty sure no matter what academy you go to; state, local, federal, you will go through something like it at least once or even multiple times. In essence, the instructors will make you exercise until you are exhausted or chase a suspect until you are exhausted. Not until you are tired, but exhausted—like when a physical trainer pushes you past your normal limits into having a dry mouth, lightheadedness, and dizzy feeling you get at the end of a real hard work out.

Once you are exhausted, they will pair you up with another classmate or an academy instructor and make you fight each other. The fight could involve boxing gloves, MMA gloves or even just grappling, but it is a wakeup call for most people who have never been hit or cracked their knuckles against someone else. It only lasts a few minutes, but it is a simulated fight for your life. Just when you think you have no energy and can't go on, they teach you your mind is very powerful and if needed, there is always a little more fight inside of you.

I went to two police academies and was involved in several "will to survive" fights. There were no ties allowed and no sandbagging with the person you go against.

Once the loser was declared either by knockout or decision, something psychologically devastating was done at both academies I went to. The instructors would take the fake gun out of the loser's holster, point it at their head and say to their face they are dead. The instructor would go on to say they are not going to ever see their kids, parents, friends, and they would show no compassion at all. This was a hard lesson but a valuable lesson. I am certain that over the years, it has helped police officers dig a little deeper when needed to win a fight. Of course, as we move forward as a country, some weak police chiefs will slowly try to get rid of this lesson, but it is very important and effective.

Regardless of the type of academy or location, the bottom line is it will prepare you to be a combination of warrior, English professor, problem solver, servant, psychologist, social worker, homeless outreach worker, and public speaker all rolled into one.

WHAT ARE SOME OF THE ASSIGNMENTS A POLICE OFFICER CAN WORK?

One of the great things about a career in law enforcement is all the fun and interesting assignments you can work. Most police officers start their careers on patrol because that is where you learn how to actually be a cop. On patrol, you learn the basics like how to use the radio, how to talk to bad guys, how to write reports, or how to make an arrest. Working patrol is where you learn the fundamentals of being a police officer. Often times, police officers choose to change assignments before they have learned enough on patrol. They, as often as not, pay the price later in their career by not knowing how to deal with criminals, or worse—they receive a promotion and forget what it was like to actually be a police officer on patrol.

Law enforcement officers are not required to promote and, in my opinion, the best cops stay at the rank of police officer. I always found it humorous when I attended a promotional ceremony for a sergeant, lieutenant, captain or even chief, and on their service record it listed only two years patrol experience. Two years may sound like enough, but keep in mind this also counts academy and FTO time, which lasts four to ten months. Agencies end up having leaders with about a year of solo patrol experience. That one year of time includes vacation and sick time so it might be 200 days of actual solo police work. A quick fix would be to mandate a specific amount of patrol time.

Once you have worked on patrol for about two to four years depending on the department, you can apply for a specialty assignment. In order to be selected for a specialty assignment, you have to be good at patrol. The types and availability of specialty assignments vary from department to department. The bigger departments boast a large selection of specialty assignments and more upward mobility, which provides a lot of opportunity. Smaller departments have fewer specialty assignments and less mobility, so there are fewer opportunities.

There are all kinds of specialty assignments such as K-9 officer, SWAT officer, undercover officer, helicopter pilot, rescue diver, flight medic, forensic computer investigator, internal affairs detective, property room officer, firearms instructor, use of force instructor, police academy drill instructor, DUI team, motor officer, search and rescue officer, public information officer, community lead officer, training and standards officer, police records officer and much, much more.

QUESTION 18
DO POLICE OFFICERS HAVE TO PASS A PHYSICAL FITNESS TEST?

Most federal agencies require initial and ongoing physical fitness tests similar to those carried out by the military. At the state, county and local level, they require you to pass a physical fitness test to be hired, but once you are off training, there is usually no annual requirement, and you can dough out as much as you choose.

I always find it disappointing that law enforcement agencies don't value the importance of physical fitness like firefighting agencies do. Firefighters have a tough job and need to be physically fit, and it is good their requisites include a strict physical fitness regimen.

Unfortunately, many law enforcement agencies are more concerned with the costs of a physical fitness program than they are about the costs of not having one. Due to this reason, police officers must take it upon themselves to maintain fitness.

As a country, if we want to help decrease the amount of force used by police officers, we need to take a more serious look at physical fitness and use of force training. When experts analyze uses of force from police, there is almost always an element of physical exhaustion, mental exhaustion, lack of confidence or all three on the part of the police officer.

It's not that police officers get into physical altercations all the time, but when they do, they must win. If a police officer loses a fight, the suspect can take their gun and kill them and anyone else around them until they are stopped.

Professional fighters know the date, time, location, rules and opponents they are going to face. The nature of law enforcement makes that impossible and a police officer must be ready to fight after eating a big meal or being on their sixth graveyard shift of the week. They don't know who they are fighting, where they are fighting, what the rules are and if the person they are fighting will be armed, but they somehow need to be ready.

Most state, county and local law enforcement agencies do not require ongoing physical fitness tests once an officer is out of the academy. There are a few departments who are trying to change things and at least provide incentives and time to work out. However, most non-federal law enforcement agencies do not require or allow police officers to work out on duty or pass an annual physical fitness test.

On the federal side, there is an annual physical fitness test similar to what the military requires, but it's not as rigorous and each federal agency sets its own standards.

Perhaps in the future things will improve, but for now, weak police leadership is perfectly content with no physical fitness requirement. So, the responsibility lands on the individual police officer to stay in shape.

If you are the wife, husband or friend of a police officer, give them support and encouragement to stay in shape. It will certainly prevent unnecessary uses of force, and may even save their life in the field.

WHAT TYPE OF TRAINING DO POLICE OFFICERS GET WHEN THEY ARE DONE WITH THE ACADEMY?

Most states have what is called a POST standard which stands for Peace Officers Standards and Training. These standards are the minimum in-service training an officer must obtain on a yearly or quarterly basis. There are a certain number of hours that must be taught to police officers on certain subjects. In California, time must be spent on use of force, driver training, firearms and racial profiling.

In addition to the state minimums, department policy will dictate how often you have to train. And like physical fitness and technology, some departments are proactive, while others only commit to the POST minimums.

Along with being sent for training, if an officer is interested in a certain area or topic, they can look for a training class and request to go to it. In some cases, they will be allowed to go on duty if budget and staffing allow. If the department won't pay for an officer to go, some will allow them to go on duty, but require them to pay for the class on their own. I think an officer having to pay for their own training is unfair but if they want to improve, they might have to do it to get better.

QUESTION 20
HOW DO YOU GET TO FLY THE POLICE HELICOPTER?

Like any cool assignment in police work, it is a competitive process for officers who already work at the agency. You must be a good police officer with experience and usually cannot apply to be a pilot from the outside the occupation. There are some exceptions with agencies hiring civilian pilots, but that is not the norm. For the agencies who do hire civilian pilots, they tend to have a police officer spotter for the police knowledge.

When there is an opening for a pilot position, a notice will go out and the selection process opens. There are things an officer can do to make themselves more qualified such as obtaining a pilot's license or having experience in the military flying helicopters. Additionally, most agencies will want you to show a genuine interest in the assignment before they open it up. As with most special assignments, police officers need to walk the fine line of showing interest and asking questions without looking like an ass-kisser.

A question I get sometimes is: "Can I fly the helicopter without working patrol?" The simple answer is no. You cannot go from Joe Citizen to helicopter pilot. At most law enforcement agencies, you must learn the job first and prove yourself on patrol before you can move into a specialty assignment.

QUESTION 21
HOW DOES A POLICE OFFICER BECOME A DETECTIVE?

At most police agencies, the first job is patrol, and after a few years, patrol officers are allowed to apply for a detective position once it opens.

Regardless of the testing process, a patrol officer will need to have a good reputation in order to get the detective assignment. Cops are inherently distrustful and tribal. At most agencies, once a cop gets certain a reputation, it follows them throughout their career. It can be improved or made worse—but overall, first impressions stick with you.

Officers who show competence, a good attitude, and the willingness to learn will help their chances. Additionally, a patrol officer can attend classes on investigations and/or do some basic investigations on "routine" report calls. For example, instead of simply writing a report about a stolen bicycle, they can do some extra digging. If there is a suspect license plate, the patrol officer can run the plate to see if they can identify a suspect. If the bike is on the high end, the patrol officer can check resale websites like Craigslist or OfferUp to see if they can find it.

Whatever the patrol officer does, they should document it in their police report, so work is not duplicated by detectives down the road. Also, by doing so, people in the agency will begin to notice. The sergeant who reviews the report, and the detective who is assigned the case will notice and (hopefully) appreciate the follow up.

QUESTION 22

HOW DOES A POLICE OFFICER GET ONTO THE SWAT TEAM?

As with any specialty assignment, the police officer must be hardworking, motivated, and a humble, street smart cop with a good attitude before they can apply.

In addition, SWAT teams and K-9 teams are very tribal and have a lot of unwritten rules an applicant needs to understand. For example, if a law enforcement agency has a healthy culture, there should be an opportunity for the specialized team to get to know the applicant prior to registration. If a police officer wants to get onto any of these coveted assignments, they need to volunteer to help whenever possible. SWAT teams often need role players who are willing to be gassed with tear gas, shot with simunitions (training ammunition), and exposed to loud concussive flashbangs. K-9 teams need agitators who are willing to put on a bite sleeve or bite suit and get their ass kicked by a police dog for a whole day of training.

Eventually, members of the SWAT team get to know the applicant and understand who they are to determine if they would be a good fit. Once the police officer meets the testing requirements, they can participate in the competitive process of being selected to the team.

Typically, the testing process will involve a review of the officer's past performance evaluations, feedback from their supervisor, a physical fitness test, a shooting test and an interview. Depending on the department, the process will vary greatly. For larger departments like LAPD, NYPD and Dallas PD, the process is very competitive and grueling. Large agencies have very busy SWAT teams and a large pool of candidates to choose from. For this reason, they are very selective, and often pick the best performing, most experienced police officers. Despite what TV, movies and the media portray, SWAT teams save lives and use great restraint. SWAT teams need someone who is intelligent and able to understand the big picture.

Once someone has been selected for a SWAT team, the journey has only just begun. Depending on the law enforcement agency, they will have to go to a basic SWAT school. After SWAT school, their training won't stop until they change assignments. They will go to breaching schools, chemical weapons schools, diversion device schools, firearms schools, and negotiation schools.

Whether SWAT is a full-time assignment or collateral duty, officers must consistently show the team they are competent enough to remain on the assignment. Even military veterans or highly successful street cops are considered rookies on the team. They will have to show humility by performing all the boring jobs that need to be done such as cleaning the SWAT van and inventorying the equipment. As they gain seniority on the team and, more importantly, trust, they will slowly move from being on an outer perimeter spot during a SWAT call to being in the stack breaching a door to arrest a bad guy.

QUESTION 23

HOW OFTEN DO POLICE OFFICERS PRACTICE SHOOTING?

There is no federal or nationwide expectation for any type of training. The frequency and focus of most training—including shooting—depends on the agency's budget, culture and state requirements. An officer involved shooting is a high risk but rare event. Since the chances of being in a shooting is low, law enforcement agencies sometimes cut corners or focus their time and budget on other types training.

It is important to differentiate between "qualifying" on the range versus actual range training. For qualifying, it involves going into a shooting range and a course of fire that requires a minimum score to pass. As for range training, it implies shooting on a range with the focus on improving your skills.

Either by necessity or culture, some agencies conduct range training as little as possible. They may make you qualify every month but don't force you to train at all. The agencies with higher budgets and competent leadership go as far as to provide range training to improve an officer's overall skills.

The department I worked for had a big budget and solid culture around range training. We were trained on things such as moving and shooting, shooting with our weak hand, shooting while using our flashlight and shooting with a gun that malfunctioned. After we trained, we would qualify on a static shooting course, which decided if we passed or failed.

Some assignments in departments are required to train and qualify more often. The obvious example of an assignment here is SWAT, but there are other assignments which—as part of their culture train extensively—such as narcotics teams or fugitive apprehension teams.

If adequate training is not provided, it is up to the individual police officer to make sure they are ready for a gun fight. Not only must they be ready to win a gunfight, but they also need to train in "shoot or don't shoot" scenarios to avoid the tragedy of accidentally shooting someone who is not a threat. The excuse of not being given time or ammo to train will mean very little to a jury if an officer accidentally shoots the wrong person. Excuses will mean even less to a killer during a gun battle if the officer can't hit their target. Therefore, I recommend significant others of police officers encourage and lend support for them to spend time and money on critical skills such as range training.

QUESTION 24

WHAT IS THE MINIMUM OR MAXIMUM AGE TO BECOME A POLICE OFFICER?

The minimum age to become a police officer or any type of law enforcement officer who carries a gun and enforces criminal law is 21 years old.

If someone is under 21, there are other ways they can work or volunteer for a law enforcement agency to get experience. Most agencies have explorer programs which allow kids to volunteer to gain experience and develop personally and professionally. The minimum age for explorer programs depends on the agency but in some cases, they allow kids as young as those in the sixth grade.

Federal agencies have age maximums, while local, county and state agencies do not. Yes, this means if someone is 65 years old and wants to become a police officer, they can. They will still need to meet the physical requirements, graduate from the police academy and complete field training. They also have to pass a pre-employment physical, and an agency (very likely) won't hire someone with pre-existing medical issues such as high blood pressure, back injuries or major surgeries. Nevertheless, if any aspiring police officer wants to join the force, nothing is impossible!

QUESTION 25

CAN YOU BE ARRESTED FOR BEING DRUNK IN PUBLIC?

It depends on where you live, but most states enforce a law which says a person can't be so intoxicated that they cannot care for their own safety. If someone is stumbling along a road and they're so drunk they fall into traffic, they'll be arrested. Or if a person is in an Uber and passes out in the car when they get to their house, they can be arrested.

Most of the time, cops don't really want to arrest a drunkard and would rather spend their time and energy going after something more worthwhile. However, if the person is a belligerent asshole, they might end up sitting in jail until they're sober enough to get home safety.

In other states, when there is not a state law, there could be a city ordinance which states being drunk in public is illegal.

One thing to note about "drunk in public arrests", is that in most states there are no requirements to give a breathalyzer test. In order to arrest someone, police officers are only required to articulate that the suspect was too drunk to care for themselves. To prove they were drunk, police officers will document the odor of an alcoholic beverage, lack of motor skills, slurred speech, blood shot eyes, a belligerent or combative attitude and even urine or vomit. You know, the stuff people do when they are too drunk to be out in public.

QUESTION 26
CAN A POLICE OFFICER COMMANDEER MY VEHICLE?

The thing I loved about being a police officer is that you can literally do anything that is "reasonable" given the information known at the time of the decision. That being said, if a police officer sees someone steal a case of beer from a liquor store it would be "unreasonable" for them to commandeer a vehicle to catch the beer thief. However, if a police officer witnessed a kidnapping of a five-year-old girl by some creep in a van, what would be "reasonable" to you?

Or what would be reasonable to a judge and to a jury under such circumstances? I am not talking about a divorced couple arguing whose day it is to have custody of their child but I mean a real kidnapping like you see in a movie.

In this scenario, with kids of my own and knowing the likely outcome of a young child being kidnapped, I would jump into the first car near me and chase after the abductor. I wouldn't care one bit about potential damage to the car I stole, because it can be replaced, but a child's life cannot.

So, yes, a police officer can commandeer a vehicle but not based on any rules or policies set by the state. The authority behind anything a police officer does is if it's considered reasonable.

Police work is not black and white, time matters, lives can be saved or lost and that is why sometimes cops get into situations which end up controversial.

64

WHY DO SO MANY LAW ENFORCEMENT OFFICERS COMPLAIN ABOUT THEIR LEADERSHIP?

I believe there is a systemic reason law enforcement agencies lack good leadership, and surprisingly, there is an easy fix of reinstating civil service protection for police chiefs. Maybe someone with some horsepower will read this and start a conversation with politicians.

Civil service protection basically means you can't get fired except for due cause. In the private sector, if you don't like someone, you can basically fire them as long as there is no discrimination involved. In government agencies good or bad, it is hard to fire anyone. Most of the time this is good for cops because their job is not to be liked but to do the right thing.

Without civil service protection, chiefs can be fired without cause. This means they must always be concerned with not losing their job not being a strong leader. As a result, this means they are controlled by the (often) <u>underwhelming</u> leadership of city council members.

Essentially, police departments can only be as "great" as the city council members who control the chief. If things go sideways—which is very common in law enforcement—the poor leadership of city councils tend to throw police chiefs under the bus. This means police chiefs are forced to be more concerned with losing their job than doing the right thing. Even chiefs with the best of intentions are overly cautious because they know they are one bad decision away from getting fired.

The easy fix is to reinstate civil service protection for police chiefs. Give them an opportunity to lead their department and do the right thing, not the action that is the least controversial or risky.

Sheriffs are elected and not appointed so they have more of an opportunity to be an actual leader and run their department autonomously. This is why you often see colorful personalities from Sheriffs because they are not one step away from being fired by a city council member.

QUESTION 28
WILL A POLICE OFFICER SHAKE MY HAND?

I am not aware of any rules which prohibit a police officer from shaking someone's hand. There are some officers who won't do it as standard practice because they think it is unsafe. In my opinion, there are benefits to shaking someone's hand and most of the time it is a good thing to do and is safe.

When I first started, the police academy taught us a person could grab your hand during a handshake and then attack you. While this is possible, it is not likely and when I was talking to someone who was not a suspect, I would shake their hand. If I was about to arrest someone or if they were a suspect, I usually didn't shake their hand.

Before body worn cameras (and to some extent, a little after the implantation of body worn cameras) we had some fun with the whole handshake thing. Whenever we had a call involving a transient, one of us would encourage the transient to shake the hand of the handling officer. Sometimes, we would go so far as to say a hug would be better, and of course, the filthier the transient, the better! Most of the time, the handling officer was able to come up with a creative excuse to get them out of it. They would say they had a cold, or got in trouble for shaking hands last week and were ordered not to do it anymore.

I know this may sound offensive, but as a police officer, you will not last without a sense of humor. We must remember that five minutes before the transient call, the officer may have been called a pig by a motorist or investigated a murder. At most agencies with healthy cultures, cops try to mess with each other in a fun way. A big, stinky hug from a transient is just one of many jokes that were played on me and my fellow officers.

QUESTION 29
WHY DO POLICE OFFICERS BREAK UP PARTIES?

I promise, it's not because the police don't like parties. Police officers break up parties or tell you to turn the music down because a neighbor has called to complain.

If you are hosting a party and want to rage all night, you can try a few tricks. First, tell your neighbors ahead of time and give them your number to text you if it gets too loud. (Or even better, invite them to the party!) If your neighbors whine and still call the police, then try to keep the doors and windows shut and the music down at a decent level. If I was to pull up on a call of people laughing and talking and the doors and windows were shut, I may not even contact the people in the "party."

If the police do knock on your door, one thing you can do is respectfully ask if the officers on scene think the noise is unreasonable. If their answer is yes, then tone all the noise down. If the officers on scene tell you they think the noise level is reasonable, then ask them if you can keep doing whatever you're doing.

On numerous occasions, I was called to "loud parties", and it was two kids playing basketball in the driveway or a family laughing and playing a board game. For those types of calls, I made sure to tell the people the noise level was not excessive, and I gave the person who called a nice "talking to".

Now, if there are 500 people playing beer pong, dancing, and swimming all while listening to music at full blast volume, I'll tell them to quiet it down (only after I get over my jealousy). If I knock on the door, and they ignore me, or worse, are "Adam Henry" AKA an asshole, then the person will suffer an earful. In my city, we had a social hosting ordinance. This means we could write an expensive ticket, based on the totality of the circumstances to the homeowner, whether they come to the door or are out of town.

CAN A POLICE OFFICER LEAVE THEIR JURISDICTION DURING A PURSUIT?

If a police officer is pursuing someone in a vehicle or on foot—yes—they can leave their jurisdiction if necessary. The police have authority throughout the state, and in some cases, even beyond state boundaries. Additionally, there are agreements or memorandums of understanding between bordering jurisdictions which allow police officers to enter and exit as needed.

Most police officers are legally allowed to make stops outside of their city for various reasons (and often do). Not only do they make random stops, but they frequently work in surrounding jurisdictions for various things. Officers could be assigned to another agency on a temporary basis, assist on a serious crime, respond when an officer needs help or patroll on account of a pre-existing agreement to share patrol jurisdictions.

There are a few exceptions when a police officer needs to stop chasing a suspect. One of these being if the suspect manages to flee the country. So, if you're are pulling a Thelma and Louise and want to make a run for it—try fleeing into Mexico or Canada. You may just get away with it. Of course, if the Federales stop you, you have a 50/50 chance of being let free or ending up in a Mexican prison with dysentery and an unwanted lover. If the Canadians catch you, they will stuff you so full of that damn Canadian bacon that you wish you had just given up. Either way, I would take my chances in the U.S.

QUESTION 31
CAN A POLICE OFFICER CARRY A GUN ON A PLANE?

Most federal law enforcement officers are specially trained and certified to carry a gun on a plane. For the most part, though, city, county and state police officers can't carry a gun on a plane.

In certain situations, such as for an investigation, training class or funeral, police officers can take a short class to be certified to carry a gun on a plane. There are obviously additional safety concerns when carrying a gun on a plane, but a gun can be carried and used on a plane, if necessary.

QUESTION 32
WHAT IS ENTRAPMENT?

Entrapment is when a police officer encourages you to do something you would otherwise not do. In plain English, this means if an undercover cop comes up to you at a bar and says he will give you a million dollars to kill his wife, and you agree, you have been entrapped. He has encouraged you to do something you were not going to do on your own.

Another example of entrapment would be if a police officer goes up to a person during a riot and hands them a rock and says, "Throw this rock at that police car." You have been encouraged to do something you were not inclined to do on your own prior to their interaction with you.

On the other hand, if you ask around a bar for someone to kill your wife and an undercover police officer says, "Sure I can do that," then you have not been entrapped. The police officer did not encourage you to do anything, he only facilitated your idea. If during the riot, a protester tells an undercover police officer to hand him a rock, and the officer hands him the rock, which he proceeds to throw, this is not be entrapment. Once again, the police officer only facilitated the protester's demand and did not encourage the protestor to do something he wasn't already planning on doing.

As evident from the examples above, entrapment is a challenging area of criminal law. Ultimately, any undercover police officer undergoes sufficient training and support to know what is allowed and what can be considered entrapment. Often times, a prosecutor will be directly involved in serious investigations to make sure the line is not crossed from good old-fashioned police work to entrapment.

QUESTION 33
ARE POLICE CARS REALLY THAT FAST?

Most police cars are purchased with what is commonly referred to as a "police package". This means they have improved suspension, better breaking, improved handling and stronger radiators in order to last longer in situations which would put a strain on a regular vehicle. However, now they are not modified to be faster than they come from the factory.

In police work, what's more important than speed is calm thinking, radios and teamwork! To a large extent, police officers catch bad guys by communicating and being calm and collected.

When a suspect runs from the police, they naturally drive above their abilities, crash and are caught. In other cases, when they get away in a police chase, there is so much technology and data available that they will eventually be identified and caught. For the lucky ones who do get away for good, chances are escaping the police isn't their first brush with the law, and it won't be their last.

QUESTION 34

WHEN CAN A POLICE OFFICER DRIVE WITH THEIR LIGHTS AND SIRENS ON?

Driving with lights and sirens is often called code-3. Most police officers are authorized to drive code-3 when they are responding to an emergency. An emergency can mean a lot of things such as a car accident, physical fight, or someone choking in a restaurant. They can also drive code-3 on a call that may turn into an "emergency" such as someone prowling in the backyard of a house. Police officers can also drive code-3 when an officer asks for urgent backup. This could mean the officer is in a fight or they can presume the situation may turn dangerous very easily.

Driving with lights and sirens doesn't mean you can go as fast as you want or do anything you please. If an officer needs help or a kid is choking, the officer will push their vehicle and driving abilities to the limit. If the call is a car accident with unknown injuries, the officer will (likely) drive code-3 at a slower speed just in case someone is injured.

QUESTION 35
DO ALL POLICE OFFICERS WEAR BULLET PROOF VESTS?

It is not a bullet proof vest; it is a ballistic vest or bullet resistant vest. Vests will only stop certain bullets, and nothing is "bullet proof" except (maybe) a military tank.

Most police departments require their officers to wear vests. Some veterans were grandfathered into the policy, which allowed vests to be optional, but as time goes on those officers are far and few in between. All in all, most police officers in uniform are wearing vests.

According to The Internation Association of Chiefs of Police, there are a total of 3,003 documented law enforcement lives saved due to the ballistic vest industry. There are a lot of fathers, brothers, husbands, wives, sisters, moms and friends who got to go home after being shot thanks to this life saving technology.

Not only can a vest save the person who is wearing it, but they also help police officers stay in the fight so he/she can stop the threat. If they don't stop the threat, the suspect is able to run loose and continue their murderous intent until someone stops them.

QUESTION 36
WHEN CAN A POLICE OFFICER FORCE THEIR WAY INTO A HOME?

To enter a house without consent, police officers must have one of the following: a warrant, exigent circumstances, or if the occupants of the house are on probation/parole and subject to search and seizure.

I am going to attempt to answer the question and give a few examples of how and when police can force entry into a home without revealing too much sensitive information.

One relatively harmless example is if someone's water pipe breaks in their bathroom and water is gushing out their front door. In this scenario, a police officer or a firefighter can kick down their front door to stop the water. If the police officer spots a kilo of cocaine on the couch, they could stay in the home. Another example would be if a person heard their neighbor scream for help and called 9-1-1. Once the police arrive, they can force their way into the house.

There are a ton of other ways the police can force entry into a home without permission, however police officers must have a strong understanding of constitutional law so they don't do anything illegal that could get them fired or sued. If a police officer forces their way into someone's home, they most likely have a good reason to do so and are acting well within the limits of the law.

ARE POLICE OFFICERS ALLOWED TO USE DISCRETION WHEN ENFORCING THE LAW?

With some laws like domestic violence or restraining orders, police officers are not allowed to use discretion or give any warnings. In general, though, the police can use discretion, but it is not always that simple. As of late, it's getting harder and harder because of body worn cameras.

The reality of police work is that sometimes doing the right thing is "not doing the right thing." One example of not doing the right thing is letting a kid with some marijuana in his pocket go with only a verbal warning. The problem with body cameras is that police officers no longer are granted the freedom of discretion. They now have to do almost everything "by the book" because they would be violating policy or even the law if they don't.

What if a police officer stopped a kid who has some marijuana? If the officer yelled at the kid and said "don't be stupid" and then threw the marijuana away, would that be allowed under policy? Probably not because you aren't allowed to yell at kids or call them stupid and you are certainly not allowed to throw the evidence of the marijuana away. If the officer writes a police report to book the marijuana into evidence, then he has to explain how he got the marijuana and who he got it from. If he did this, the person he found it on would be labeled as a "suspect."

When I started, we would yell at the kid, maybe take him home to his parents and throw the marijuana into a gutter or trashcan. Now days, body cameras and social justice warriors have taken away the discretion of police officers. People are being charged with minor crimes that they would not have had on their permanent record. Sometimes the best of intentions results in the worst of consequences.

The discretion that is thankfully still allowed is the ability to *choose* to write a driving ticket or not. It is illegal to drive without a license, and in some states not only can you get a ticket, but you can be arrested and potentially your vehicle impounded. During my 20 years as a police officer (including time as a motorcycle officer), I pulled over a lot of Hispanic gardeners and construction workers for minor traffic violations. Some of them did not have driver's licenses because they were illegal aliens. It bothered me that they were in our country illegally. It was frustrating that they didn't have a driver's license or insurance. However, I put myself in their shoes and thought about what I would do if I were them. As I stood at their car window, I remembered they were out working very hard and needed their truck for work. I thought about how it was unfair that if they got into an accident, the others drivers' insurance would need to cover the cost of the repair. I remember the time I was hit by an unlicensed and uninsured driver. But what good would giving them a citation and towing their car do? With all those thoughts running through my mind, as long as they were respectful and didn't have any warrants, I would only give them a warning.

The fact that I let them go may infuriate some people, but if I towed their truck, again, what good would it do to that person? They wouldn't leave the country and they couldn't go out and get a license and insurance.

These examples are just the tip of the iceberg in the complicated job of being a police officer. It is often an emotional struggle to do the right thing when enforcing the law. Most good cops do tend to bend the rules when trying to do the right thing.

87

QUESTION 38

WHY DO POLICE OFFICERS CHASE A SUSPECT IN A CAR FOR HOURS INSTEAD OF JUST RAMMING IT TO END THE PURSUIT?

I assure you, police officers pursuing a suspect want nothing more than to ram, P.I.T. or block the suspect in order to stop them. The officer's hands are probably tied by weak leadership. Depending on the traffic conditions and the speed of the pursuit, suspects could easily be stopped safely with a variety of techniques such as ramming, boxing in or the P.I.T. maneuver. However, officers are forced to chase them for sometimes hours.

Police chiefs, directors and some sheriffs are too fearful of being sued, and possibly the loss of their job so they do not allow techniques that could safely end the pursuit.

The irony here is there are a lot of short police pursuits that end early because the police intervene with their patrol car. The problem is, these chases don't last long enough for the news helicopter to pick up. The result is only the long clown car chases make it onto the TV, thereby feeding into the popular narrative that police can't do anything to stop fleeing cars.

QUESTION 39
HOW DO I GET OUT OF A DUI IF I AM PULLED OVER?

Driving under the influence, or "DUI" as it is often called, is one of the more difficult crimes to get out of during a traffic stop. If I was a defense attorney and wanted to help you get out of being arrested for DUI, it would be very difficult. Organizations like Mothers Against Drunk Driving (MADD) work hard to make sure DUIs are easy to enforce and impossible for people to get away with. This is because a lot of people are killed every year from drunk driving crashes. According to the National Highway Traffic Safety Administration (NHTSA), in 2023, an estimated 13,000-13,500 people died in impaired driving vehicle collisions. By comparison, according to the FBI, 18,456 people were murdered in the United States in the same time frame.

There really is no way to effectively get out of a DUI once you are pulled over. I have heard or tried all the so called "tricks". When I was a patrol cop, I had to attend different DUI training classes. Most cops, including myself, goofed around at training when we could. This means we did anything and everything to try and deceive the breathalyzers or somehow trick the testing machines. We could never get anything to make the chemical tests inaccurate. Although, at times we got the test to shut down and make an error, but none of what we did would help if you get pulled over. If the testing machine failed to show a result, there are things a police officer can do to legally arrest someone without a valid chemical test.

People often try to avoid rolling down their window, suck on a penny and/or candy before the breathalyzer, or claim they have a head injury. However, once they get pulled over, the police officer is going to be able to tell if they are drunk because of the training involving DUIs.

If you are drunk and get pulled over, I would advise you to be as cooperative as possible. Perhaps the district attorney or judge will show some mercy for your case. It does nobody any good if you are a total asshole, so act accordingly.

As I write this, I must admit, I drove drunk more times than I should have as a teen, and even during my first couple of years as a police officer. Heck, I still mess up and do it from time to time, so I am not ignorant about the power of alcohol.

QUESTION 40
CAN POLICE OFFICERS FIRE A WARNING SHOT?

It depends on the department's policy, but yes, it is allowed under certain circumstances. There are not a lot of real-world examples of warning shots because of the various dangers and general lack of public support involved in firing a gun. In fact, I never heard of a warning shot in all my years of service, but there are situations when it could be an effective tactic.

Let's say there was a large fight outside of a night club with a large crowd and there was only one police officer in the area. As the police officer arrived, he saw a man on the ground being repeatedly kicked in the head by three unarmed men. Although the police officer could be justified in shooting one (or perhaps all the men) who were trying to kill the young man on the ground, it would not work out well if the officer did in fact shoot the suspects.

In this case, the officer would be legally and morally justified in firing warning shots. Of course, the public would freak out, weak leaders would throw the officer under the bus and some cops with practically no patrol time would say how they could have handled it better. However, the victim would be safe, no one would be dead and the crowd would run away.

Unfortunately, I don't think an officer these days would feel comfortable firing the warning shots and the victim would instead end up seriously injured or even dead. This is a perfect example of why support from the public and leadership is imperative. With support, police can do a lot of good even if it requires firing warning shots to make suspects run away.

QUESTION 41
CAN POLICE OFFICERS PUNCH SOMEONE?

Yes, police officers can use force to effect an arrest, overcome resistance and prevent escape. The force committed must objectively be reasonable given the facts known to the officer at the time of the incident and not with the benefit of hindsight. The Supreme Court has said that any reasonable force is allowed, so a police officer can punch your face, kick you in the balls, or even pick up a rock and throw it at you, so long as it is reasonable.

Although force looks ugly, and the media plays it over and over, it is perfectly legal and ethical to do so under the right circumstances. When I was a cop, I arrested plenty of suspects who would not follow my lawful commands. In those situations, if I could not use my strength to force their hands behind their backs, I would have to punch them in the body (or face) to get them to submit to my arrest.

I remember my partner Tony and I wrestling with a burglary suspect and trying to get him into handcuffs. The suspect was much stronger than both of us and we could not get the cuffs on him. After struggling for about a minute to pull his hands behind his back, and giving verbal warnings, I punched the suspect square in his nose. Although my punch was nothing special, he stopped what he was doing and said,

"You can't hit me." We told him again to put his hands behind his back, but he started to resist again so I warned him and then hit him in the nose a second time. Once again, the suspect said, "You can't hit me," but he was so surprised that I had hit him, we were able to safely put him in handcuffs.

Hitting someone as a distraction may come across as a brutal tactic, but it is nearly impossible to get someone in handcuffs by simply pulling their hands behind their back. If you don't believe me, I offer you to try it one day. Set it up as an exercise with a few friends and make them try to hold your hands behind your back for at least ten seconds to simulate the time it would take to put one handcuff on. If you resist, there is no way to get handcuffs on someone without seriously outnumbering them.

We are a nation of laws, and the Supreme Court has determined that just because someone doesn't want to be arrested, it doesn't give them the right to resist. Reasonable force, including punching, can be used if the officer can articulate why it was necessary. I'm not saying that police should be allowed to punch anyone for anything, but there are times when it is the right thing to do.

If a person feels they are being unfairly arrested or detained, the best thing they can do is submit to the arrest. After they are arrested, there are a lot of safeguards in place which protect their rights, including having their day in court. Resisting arrest on the spot or running away because of fear only makes the situation worse, as it risks someone getting hurt or killed.

QUESTION 42

WHAT SHOULD I DO IF I GET PULLED OVER TO HELP MAKE THE STOP AS SAFE AS POSSIBLE?

Pull over as soon as it is safe to the right side of the road. If you are on the freeway or there is no safe area to pull over, put your turn signal on, slow down and show the officer you are trying to pull over. Most police officers will recognize that you're making a conscious effort to make things safe and sound.

Once you have pulled over, turn off your car, and if it is nighttime, turn on your interior lights. If you have a dark tint, roll all your windows down. Put your hands somewhere visible; on the steering wheel or knees, and if you are a passenger, wait until the officer approaches the car. Do not leave the car unless instructed to do so.

Don't move or reach for anything until the officer asks you to. Also, follow the officer's commands. The Supreme Court has recognized the danger of "routine traffic stops" and ruled that police officers can order any and all occupants out of a vehicle and detain them as long as it is necessary to complete their investigation. The more heated you get, the more dangerous the stop. When it is all over, whether you get a warning, ticket or arrested, you will have your day in court. You will even have a chance to file a complaint if you think that is necessary.

However, arguing or resisting during the traffic stop is pointless and dangerous for everyone involved.

QUESTION 43
CAN I SHOOT SOMEONE WHO BREAKS INTO MY HOME?

Before answering this question, keep in mind that I am not a lawyer; I am not a prosecutor; I am not a defense attorney, and I can only give you what I know based on my background as a police officer. There are classes offered by more intelligent experts in this area—and I strongly recommend if you own a gun, that you take one.

In most circumstances, you legally can shoot a home intruder. Self-defense of yourself or another person is a God given right and is supported by our constitution and most of our laws.

Let's first discuss the legal aspects of the question. In all 50 states, you are legally allowed to use force, which includes *lethal* force, if you feel you or another person is in danger of serious bodily injury or death. Essentially, you must be in fear for your life. There is an assumption in our constitution and case law which claims that your home is your "castle". On top of constitutional and case law, most state laws presume that if someone is breaking into your home, they are doing so with the intent to seriously injure or kill. As a result—with this assumption present in most states—there is no need for you to wait to determine the intruder's intentions before you shoot them.

Usually, you cannot shoot an intruder you catch breaking into your house who is running away. It is hard to prove you were afraid for your life if the suspect is running away from the scene when you shoot them. It might be human nature to want to shoot the intruder, but again, you must prove you were in fear for your life.

What makes this question difficult is there are situations where you would absolutely be justified shooting an intruder who is running away from the scene. For instance, let's say the very same burglar stole your loaded shotgun from under your bed and was running towards your neighbor's door. In this scenario, you could shoot them, and it would be justified. You knew the shotgun was loaded and you would be in fear for your neighbor's life—regardless of the burglar's intentions.

In any shooting, the facts of the encounter will first be reviewed by officers on the scene, then by detectives, and lastly, a district attorney. If you ever use force to defend yourself, you will need to explain why you did. When the police show up, it would be good idea to ask for an attorney before you answer any questions, but in some cases, it might be hard. There are things you might want to say to capture your mindset. For example, if it was past midnight and the burglar had a hammer in hand and swung it at your wife, you would likely want to mention that. Statements regarding your mindset will be used for or against you. There is no one right answer, so that is why an attorney can help you.

If there was a mistake and perhaps you shot the burglar that you should not have, do not lie. This is the worst thing you can do because you will get caught, and you will lose all credibility and be prosecuted. Instead, explain your state of mind at the time. Your state of mind is a very powerful piece of evidence and is frequently used in fatal incidents. If you appear to be credible, then the officers, the district attorney and (possibly) a jury will consider what you were feeling at the time.

Now that we understand the legal aspects of shooting a burglar, I am going to talk about the emotional, financial, social, and political issues you will face if you shoot another person. Although it should not be a factor when you or your family are in danger, these things need to be in the back of your mind. Notwithstanding total justification for the act, you will need to consider what your heart, your neighbors, your coworkers, the media, politicians, political activists, special interest groups and even your own family and friends will think of you. Yes, that's correct, if your life is on the line, this should also be in the back of your mind.

If you shoot an intruder and live in a republican county or state, you likely won't be as scrutinized as you would be in a democratic county or state. For example, if you are living in a democratic city like New York, the district attorney (and unfortunately even the police chief) may try to take advantage of the tragedy and prosecute you just to make an example of your situation or to promote their own agenda.

Regardless of where you live or what I have to say on the matter, when it comes to an intruder, you should come to your own conclusion, because in the end, it is your responsibility to protect your home.; Not me, not the media, not politicians, only you.

In closing, here is quote I heard countless times over my career that may help you in a life-or-death situation: "It is better to be judged by 12 than carried by 6."

QUESTION 44
WHY DO POLICE CARS HAVE AR-15'S IN THEM?

As a cop, a lot of people in sunny southern California would ask me this question. If someone asked me, I would take the time to explain that police officers need to have better weapons and training so they can win any fight they engage in. I would tell them that if a call of a shooting came over the radio, police might need AR-15s to gain the upper hand in a gunfight (or at least match the suspects firepower). In the past, a shotgun was the go-to weapon for police officers, and in certain engagements, it still is. However, the AR-15 is a very accurate and very powerful tool for police officers.

There will always be evil people determined to kill as many people as they can during a shooting rampage. These evil people, whether they are terrorists or mentally unstable monsters, make thorough plans and even train on the range with the weapons prior to their rampage. In any circumstance, the cops need to win the gunfight every time. In order to win, cops need the best weapons and training there are.

QUESTION 45

DO POLICE OFFICERS RACIALLY PROFILE?

I won't pretend that in the past, police didn't racially profile, but police officers today do not. However, I am going to be straight with you and tell you the realities of police work, not just a politically correct version of something you want to hear.

In the United States, racial profiling is illegal and prohibited by all police departments across the nation; It is not socially acceptable and does not happen. What is encouraged, however, is finding things that are out of place because the same thing an ordinary citizen may look twice at is the same thing a diligent cop should investigate.

Although police officers don't racially profile, they do "dirtbag profile". This means if a suspect looks like a gangbanger and walks through a retirement community, they will likely be stopped. If it turns out they're visiting their grandma, then there is no harm, no foul. In fact, even gangbangers expect to get stopped when they look the part outside of their normal neighborhood.

Police officers are well trained and experienced at examining situations and finding things that seem out of place. For a cop, it's a bit like the book series *Where's Waldo?* However, instead of looking at a page in the book, cops drive their beat and try to find the real-life things that appear unusual. Often times, when things are out of place, it just means the police officer needs to dig a little deeper. That may mean turning around and running a license plate or just taking a second glance at something or someone. It is the little things that police officers notice, such as a rental car with four guys in it who refuse to make eye contact, or a guy wondering around the neighborhood in gym clothes, but with no gym bag or sweat.

WHY DO I GET PULLED OVER SO MUCH?

Well, if you really do get pulled over "a lot" there are a few possible reasons. It may be because you drive a car that has glaring vehicle code violations like broken taillights or a smashed windshield; It may be that you live in a high crime area and the police are being proactive and making a lot of investigatory traffic stops; It may be because you live in a low crime area and since there is not a lot going on, the proactive cops make lots of stops, in an effort to find a criminal or make an arrest.

The Supreme Court has ruled the subjective reason for the stop is not relevant, as long as there is a lawful reason to stop you. You can equate this to fishing. The best cops make a ton of lawful stops in the hopes of finding a criminal.

Oh, one last thing. You may get pulled over because you look like an "Adam Henry" AKA asshole.

Regardless of the reason why you get stopped, if you feel you are innocent and should not have been stopped, you can ask the cops why you were stopped. The police officer should be able to tell you. If they are rude or do something wrong, follow their commands, and when it is all over—if you still feel the process was not right—you can call and speak to their supervisor and/or file a complaint.

QUESTION 47
DO POLICE OFFICERS HAVE A QUOTA?

No, they do not. Quotas have been determined by the courts to be unfair, unethical and illegal. However, like most police work, there is a gray area I will try to explain.

Although quotas are not allowed, what is permitted is the expectations or comparisons among peers. For example, if eight out of nine police officers on a shift write between five and ten tickets a month, then that would be considered the shift average. If an officer on that shift writes no tickets for three months in a row, they may get talked to about their performance.

The number of tickets a police officer writes is not necessarily a good indicator of how good of a cop they are, but at the end of the day, a police officer must show they have done something with their time. If they don't like writing tickets, they can make arrests, walk on foot and talk to business owners or visit kids at schools, etc. All these activities are tracked in one way or another and a competent supervisor knows if a police officer is working hard.

Peer pressure is also a good corrector of bad behavior in the law enforcement culture. If the boss doesn't notice an officer being lazy, the officers on the shift will. They will handle it informally and make sure the behavior is corrected to match the culture of the department.

QUESTION 48

CAN A POLICE OFFICER SHOOT AN UNARMED SUSPECT?

Yes, police officers can shoot someone if they don't have a weapon. The Supreme Court (and most department policies) require a police officer to be in fear of great bodily injury or death to themselves or a third party. I will list a few examples to help you understand when and how a police officer might feel in danger of great bodily injury or death, even if the suspect does not have a gun.

A police officer can legally and morally shoot an unarmed MMA fighter who is attacking them; A police officer can legally and morally shoot two suspects who attempt to attack them on a rural highway with no backup around; A police officer can legally and morally shoot a suspect who is trying to pull another officer's gun out of their holster; A police officer can legally and morally shoot a suspect who is trying to choke them or punch them in the face while they are wrestling on the ground.

When deciding to shoot someone, the issue is not whether there is a weapon, but if the amount of force is reasonable. I worked with some pretty tough cops who would probably not be justified in shooting an MMA fighter. I also worked with smaller officers who would be legally and morally justified in using lethal force due to their difference in size, strength and skill.

Every use of force must be gauged objectively by a reasonable officer under similar circumstances without the benefit of hindsight. The standard for force is not specific to a type of weapon or skill but needs to consider the totality of the circumstances. If it is reasonable, a police officer can shoot, stab, bludgeon, choke, eye gouge, run over or drown a suspect but they will have to answer as to why they turned to lethal force.

QUESTION 49
WHY DO COPS SHOOT SUSPECTS IN THE CHEST INSTEAD OF AIMING FOR THE LEG?

When lethal force is justified, the quickest and safest way to stop a threat is to shoot at the biggest target which also has the best chance of stopping them. For us humans, this is the torso which is also referred to as center mass. In movies, police officers sometimes aim for the leg or kneecap but in real life with fatigue, adrenaline, sweat, tunnel vision, anger, fear and blood, the safest and most effective part to aim for is the body.

Aiming for the biggest target not only helps ensure a stray bullet doesn't travel down the street and hit an innocent person, but it also ensures the threat will stop as quickly as possible. If someone is high on drugs or adrenaline, a shot to the arm or leg might never stop them but a shot to the heart, lungs or any other vital organ would stop them no matter how juiced up they were at the time.

Can a police officer who is a good shot aim for the arm or leg in certain circumstances and probably hit it? Yes, but it is much safer to fire at the chest than a limb to stop the suspect.

IF POLICE OFFICERS ARE THE GOOD GUYS, THEN WHY ARE THERE SO MANY BAD POLICE SHOOTINGS?

Math does not have emotions. If you look at the statistics behind police shootings, the fact is the number of unjustified shootings is rather small. However, when the news plays thes unjustified shootings over and over, and with celebrities and athletes focusing on them, it appears as though there is a real problem.

Depending on what source you cite, it is estimated that police officers in the United States conduct over 50 million contacts with people every year. These contacts include traffic stops, arrests, warrants, investigations, report calls, pedestrian stops, fights, arguments, casual conversations, etc.

The Washington Post has a very good comprehensive database about police shootings in the United States. According to The Washington Post, there are around 1,000 officers involved in shootings per year. Mathematically, if you take the number of shootings in context with the amount of police contacts, this means your chances of being shot by the police in a justified shooting is .00002%.

Let's say half of these shootings were unjustified, this would mean your chance of being unjustifiably shot by a police officer is .00001%.

For all the energy and media coverage that goes into police shootings, let's look at some other ways you can die and their related percentages:

- The chance of you dying in a car crash is a <u>thousand times more likely</u> at .009%.
- The chance of you dying from a bee sting is <u>five times more likely</u> at .00005%.
- The chance of you dying from a lightning strike is <u>eight times as likely</u> at .000083%.
- The chance of you dying from heat exposure is <u>seventy times more likely</u> at .00007%.

The statistics above prove there is an *exaggeration* on the coverage of unjustified police shootings. When is the last time the media ran stories over and over about bee stings deaths and the need to do something about them? Or how about heat exposure deaths or lighting strikes on video loop with town hall meetings, outraged citizens and demand for change?

The Squatter's Rights

When the Enemy Moves In – and the
Battle to Reclaim What Belongs to God

Dr. Giovanna L. Sanders, Bishop
Dennis Sanders

Crowned Warrior Publishing

Contents

1. A Note to the Reader   1

Prologue   5
Pay Attention to What's Happening Across the Street

2. SECTION 1: FINDING THE KEYS   8
Authority, Identity, and What Was Left Behind

3. The Squatter's Tale   15
When Occupation Is Mistaken for Ownership

4. The House of Horrors   20
What Neglect Looks Like from the Inside

5. The Resistance   24
When Wanting Help Isn't Enough

6. The Return of the Squatter   29
When Surrender Is Only Temporary

7. The Survey   33
When Purpose Determines What Must Be Removed

8. The Key   37
Authority Exists—Whether It Is Exercised or Not

9. The Demolition   40
From Ruin to Solid Ground

10. SECTION 2: A GUIDED DEBRIEF   44
     An Invitation to Look Again

11. Guided Debrief I: When Absence Becomes Access   47

12. Guided Debrief II: When Access Becomes Occupation   57

13. Guided Debrief III: When the House Is Left Empty   64

14. Guided Debrief IV: When Authority Is Challenged   69

15. Guided Debrief V: Removal, Replacement, and Solid   74
     Ground

16. SECTION 3: FOUNDATIONS FOR FREEDOM   81
     Understanding Access, Ownership, and the Need for De-
     liverance

17. Salvation: Who Owns the House?   97
     Why Ownership Determines Authority

18. Deliverance: Enforcing What Ownership Secured   107
     How Authority Is Exercised Through Language

19. Closing Chapter   117
     When the Ground Is Finally Solid

20. Continue the Journey   123

About the authors   124

Chapter One

A Note to the Reader

Trauma spares no one. It does not distinguish between belief and disbelief, certainty or doubt. Pain, loss, grief, and disruption visit every life in one form or another. No worldview, faith system, or personal philosophy offers immunity from suffering. This is not a statement of belief—it is a statement of the human condition.

This book is written through the lens of two people who use the Bible as their compass. That lens does not exempt us—or anyone else—from pain. It does not prevent trauma, addiction, or loss. What it does offer is a way of understanding what suffering leaves behind and how people attempt to survive it. Whether one believes in God, questions His existence, or rejects faith altogether, the impact of trauma is the same: something is altered, something is left exposed, and something must be clung to in order to keep going.

Throughout these pages, Scripture shapes the way experiences are interpreted—not as a religious exercise, but as a framework that has helped us make sense of what pain opens the door to and what it takes to reclaim what is lost. Readers who do not share our faith may still recognize the patterns described here: withdrawal after loss, avoidance as self-protection, and the slow way unaddressed pain can take up more space than intended. The language may differ, but the experience is shared.

This story is not written to divide believers from non-believers, but to confront a reality common to all: what we do with trauma matters. What we ignore does not disappear. And what we allow to linger often begins to shape us. Survival is not determined by belief alone, but by how pain is handled and where hope is placed when life becomes unbearable.

Of course, the hope we carry—and the solution we believe in—is found in Christ. We do not shy away from that, nor do we impose it. The choice of what to believe, and when, ultimately belongs to you, the reader. The purpose of this book is not to pressure or persuade through fear or religious language, but to talk honestly about deliverance in a way that is accessible and grounded in real experience. For those who desire it, prayers are provided at the end of the book as a gentle offering, not an obligation. Whether you share our faith or not, you are invited to continue this journey—to observe, to reflect, and to consider what freedom might look like in your own life.

This book is written from two distinct but complementary perspectives.

We share this story through lived experience and pastoral insight. One voice reflects what we believe the Holy Spirit revealed in real time as the events of the story unfolded. The other writes from the role of an ordained minister, offering theological grounding and guiding readers through the structured debriefs in the latter portion of the book. Together, these perspectives are offered to present the fullest picture possible—shared with honesty, humility, and faithfulness.

To help orient the reader, this book is divided into **three sections**, each serving a distinct purpose.

Section One tells the story. It invites the reader into a lived experience—unfiltered, honest, and reflective—allowing space for recognition, resonance, and understanding.

Section Two provides guided debriefs. This section slows the pace and offers pastoral insight, Scripture, and structured reflection to help process what has been presented and to ground the narrative in biblical truth.

Section Three offers clarity and understanding. Here, we address foundational concepts such as boundaries, access, salvation, and deliverance. This section is intended to provide language, order, and perspective—especially for readers who may be encountering these ideas for the first time.

Each section builds upon the last. Together, they are designed not only to tell a story, but to help the reader discern what belongs, what does not, and how restoration and freedom are possible through Christ.

Therefore, read on with honesty and courage. Ask the questions that have gone unspoken and consider the doors you may have locked—not to hide, but to survive—and what it might mean to open them now with intention. Freedom is not reckless, nor is it a luxury;

it is rightful. It is our prayer that these pages prepare the ground for your freedom.

Courage does not require the absence of fear; sometimes the bravest choice is simply to do it afraid.

Prologue

$\mathbf{M}$y husband and I have the privilege of serving as senior pastors of a wonderful church nestled in a residential neighborhood in an average American city. A few years ago, an unexpected opportunity arose—a piece of property across the street from our church became available for purchase. The timing couldn't have been better, as our growing congregation had outgrown our parking lot, and this acquisition would provide the much-needed space to expand.

However, as we moved forward with the decision to buy, my husband discovered that a squatter had taken residence in the home on the property. When we met him that afternoon—a man whom, for the sake of this book, we will call "Joey"—we left the meeting unsure of our next steps. He disclosed being addicted to drugs and wanting whatever help we could offer him. However, his spiritual condition was equally as concerning as his physical one and my husband and I were somewhat perplexed as to what to do next.

As my husband and I crossed the street and headed back to the church office, the words of his story gripped my mind. His backstory was horrific and his fight for survival was heartbreaking. As I stood there, staring through the church office window, with tears streaming down my face overwhelmed with the sadness of his story, I heard the Holy

Spirit speak clearly to my heart: "Pay attention to what's happening across the street."

I knew from experience that when the Holy Spirit speaks, He is revealing something deeper. "What do You mean?" I asked. Again, He repeated, "Pay attention to what's happening across the street." But this time, something more came with it—the title of this book, "The Squatter's Rights". Over the next several weeks, as we finalized the purchase and prepared to clear the property, the message of this book was impressed upon my heart, piece by piece.

What I am about to share with you is exactly what the Lord revealed to me during that journey—insights that go far beyond a simple land acquisition. This story explains what happens when an intruder moves in, unwanted, unwelcomed and starts taking possession of what does not belong to them. What happens when the rightful owner returns, only to find their home occupied by a force that refuses to leave? It is our prayer that as you turn these pages, the Holy Spirit will open your eyes to the places in your life where the enemy has taken up residence and refuses to leave. May this true story serve as a catalyst for your deliverance and freedom.

This book is not just about Joey—a real man whose life has been shaped by trauma, addiction, and despair. It is a type and shadow unfolding of events about a spiritual reality that many fail to recognize: when darkness gains access to a life, it does not surrender easily. The territory claimed isn't going to be returned without a fight. Just as a squatter refuses to leave a house without a legal battle, demonic forces do not willingly give up the ground they have claimed in a person's soul.

Joey's story is more than a tragic tale of addiction and brokenness; it is a warning. The house he occupies is a symbol of any individual, Christian or otherwise, that has opened the door of their life thereby granting access to the enemy to come in and claim authority in that space. The house across the street represents the battle between good and evil that wages over every soul. The pastors want to help, but the hold of addiction—like the grip of spiritual bondage—is not easily broken. As the battle intensifies, Joey, much like those trapped in sin, finds himself unable or unwilling to leave, even when faced with consequences.

As the story of this unforeseen physical squatter unfolds, we will explore the dangerous reality of spiritual squatters—how sin, addiction, and demonic influences creep in through open doors of trauma, compromise, and neglect. We will examine what happens when the enemy establishes a foothold and refuses to leave, and, most importantly, how true freedom can only come when the rightful owner—the One who paid for our redemption—steps in to reclaim what is His.

This is a true story of warning, but also of hope. If you have ever struggled with spiritual bondage, if you have ever felt powerless against the strongholds in your life, then let this book be your guide. Because no matter how long darkness has occupied a place, the light always has the power to drive it out.

Chapter Two

SECTION 1: FINDING THE KEYS

I could only assume that, during the construction of this typical "American dream" house, the architects imagined the years it would stand. The house had darling character, with a large yard and a spattering of annuals and perennials gracing the landscape. But slowly, the charm began to diminish as chipped paint and debris replaced the colors of nature.

This house didn't fall into ruin overnight. And honestly, even at the end of it's life, from the outside, things didn't appear to be totally out of control. Sure, a little unkempt; that part was obvious. But there was no way of knowing the reality of what was going on inside.

The house

Its story began with an unexpected tragedy—the loss of a loved one. The grieving spouse, unable to bear the painful memories within its walls, made the difficult decision to leave it all behind. Renting out the property seemed like the best option, as the weight of staying was too much to bear. Eventually, the owner couldn't even drive past it. What was once meant to be a home filled with love, children, and the beautiful privilege of creating memories became a painful monument to what was lost.

Pain has a way of convincing us that distance is wisdom. Sometimes it is—but often it's just avoidance dressed up as survival. Walking away may explain why something was left unattended, but it doesn't change what happens next. What isn't faced doesn't stay neutral. It keeps working, whether we're present or not. Decay is not instant. It implies a slow change from a state of soundness or perfection.

Trauma, in any form, often acts as an "open door" for the enemy to enter. In this case, overwhelming grief caused life as the owner knew it to come to a halt. While she physically closed the door to her own presence in the house, she unknowingly opened it to others. Her absence left the home vulnerable, and as renters—and in some cases, invaders—came and went, destruction followed. Without someone to truly care for and protect it, the house fell into the hands of those who would only bring harm. The moment access was granted to the wrong occupants, decline became inevitable.

Authority doesn't disappear just because we're tired of exercising it. When responsibility is set down—out of grief, exhaustion, or delay—something else will step in to fill the gap. This isn't dramatic or sudden. It's practical. What isn't managed doesn't wait patiently to be reclaimed.

Over the years, the house saw its share of tenants—some transient, others who left a deeper mark. In the beginning, each new renter arrived with a promise of renewal. Fresh coats of paint, patched-up windows, and new furnishings hinted at potential. Freshly planted flowers sat in colorful pots adorning the front porch, and wind chimes harmonized with the birds in the air. However, the work was always short-lived. Like clockwork, resolve would falter, and before long, the house's outward decay would begin again.

After watching this pattern unfold for over a decade, I don't believe there was malice in the heart of the the tenants. Some simply lacked the resources or skill to maintain the property. Others seemed to lack the will. Over time, the house became a reflection of its residents' struggles—a sad mirror of lives that were rarely able to sustain the hope they brought with them.

As time went on, things took a darker turn. The police, once rare visitors, became regular ones. The backyard—once a place where children might have played or families gathered—devolved into an overgrown field where chickens, ducks, and other random animals roamed freely. The daily smell of burning rancid items filled the air. The chaotic rhythm of the home was accompanied by a parade of unfamiliar faces—people coming and going, none of them seeming to have any genuine purpose other than to satisfy some unspoken need.

But there was something more to the house now. An unsettling stillness had settled in—a silence that felt too heavy, too thick. Traffic slowed, and in its place, an ominous presence seemed to hover around the building, almost as if it were waiting for something.

There's a difference between things being broken and things being bound. Broken things can be repaired. Bound things settle in when neglect becomes normal and boundaries stop being enforced. Darkness doesn't rush—it waits until disorder feels familiar and intervention feels inconvenient.

It was when a neighbor shared the news that things began to make sense. The renter, once a shadow in the house, had suddenly passed away. The news came as a shock. I had just seen him days earlier, smoking his daily cigarette by the makeshift garden he had tended for months. I could smell the smoke wafting from his front porch through the church office windows. He had always been friendly, though never quick to accept the many church invitations extended his way. Now, there would be no more hellos exchanged. The patriarch figure of the household was gone.

Yet it wasn't the shock of his passing that lingered—it was the aftermath of what followed.

The neighbor informed my husband that the remaining occupants—those tethered to the house in one way or another—had begun hastily packing their belongings, leaving behind pets and trash, abandoning everything that once seemed important. The dogs were left behind—the only living creatures remaining in the house—sickly and disoriented. They pushed against the boundaries of their confinement, clawing at the air, trying to make sense of their new reality.

This particular family had moved out during "non-working hours". They made their transition during the cloak of the night. We would not have known the full extent of the activity taking place, but our neighbor had watched it all unfold through her kitchen window. All we knew was there was non-stop smoke fire that seemed to be present in the yard. But that was not unusual for this group. To us, although the traffic had slowed down, things still appeared *normal*.

The house, now vacant, was more than a physical space—it had become a tomb. What had once been bad had now morphed into something far worse. The smell of neglect lingered. The walls seemed to close in. Windows were cracked. Floorboards creaked under the weight of past decisions. A brooding darkness filled the rooms.

Something had changed, and it wasn't just the house.

What the owner did not know was the condition the house had fallen into. She had not set foot inside it for years. She did not even have keys to enter it herself. Grief had driven her away, and time had done the rest. When my husband contacted her after learning of the tenant's death, she was stunned by what she heard. She had never imagined the home had deteriorated to this extent. When he asked if she would consider selling the property, she agreed and gave us permission to enter and assess it.

When my husband walked through the house alone for the first time, he was unprepared for what he found. That day, he encountered no one living there. However, what he did see was wiring and plumbing that had been stripped from the walls. Trash filled the rooms. But buried beneath the debris were fragments of lives once lived there—family photographs still pinned to the walls, children's drawings, birth certificates, Social Security cards. Pieces of identity abandoned alongside the destruction, as though the stories attached to them had been discarded as well.

As he sorted through the debris, he came across something unexpected: a set of keys.

When he tried them in the locks, he realized they belonged to the house. It was a miracle that he found them to begin with. The mounds of trash were everywhere and the fact he saw them was in itself unbelievable. But I have a feeling this was a God wink that kept building the puzzle of this story before we even knew we had a story to retell.

We had permission. We had access. We had the keys.

Having the keys doesn't mean the space will be surrendered politely. Restored authority is often met with resistance—not because the claim is legitimate, but because it's gone unchallenged for too long. Recognition is the beginning. Enforcement is what actually changes things.

What we did not yet know was that someone else believed a claim had already been made—and in the days that followed, we would learn that possession does not always yield willingly, even when authority is legitimate.

Chapter Three

The Squatter's Tale

Our church had been growing steadily for the last decade. It was a blessing—but with growth came challenges. The parking lot that once felt ample was now overflowing, forcing churchgoers to park several blocks away. The need for more space had become pressing, yet expansion felt impossible. The land surrounding the church was locked in place, and every option seemed closed.

Then, across the street, a solution began to reveal itself.

Unfortunately, it came at a cost.

The house had slowly become a neighborhood eyesore over the years, but this time something felt different. It was sobering to realize that tragedy had become the catalyst for what looked like an answered prayer. As we learned more about the situation, it almost felt too good to be true. There was a quiet, undeserved sense of guilt that accompanied the possibility—we stood to benefit from another layer of loss tied to that property's history. The house itself wasn't the goal; it was the land that held the promise of expansion.

Sometimes opportunity arrives wrapped in discomfort. Not every open door feels clean or celebratory. That doesn't mean it isn't legitimate—it means it comes with responsibility. Favor doesn't erase complexity, and growth often requires decisions that feel heavier than expected.

A great deal hinged on acquiring the property. After receiving the owner's permission to assess the house, my husband asked me to walk across the street with him.

"Come with me," he said. "I want you to walk through it with me...at least take a look inside."

We approached cautiously, our eyes scanning the structure. As I neared the yard, I could see a smoldering fire in a makeshift fire pit. I remember thinking it strange given this house was supposed to be empty. Had the previous renters returned to clean up the mess they had left behind?

It was immediately clear this wasn't simply a house in need of renovation. The smell reached us the closer we got to the house—decay, rot, and human disregard layered thick in the air. The smoke curling persistently from that fire pit in the backyard was carrying the strange, nauseating scent of burning refuse—dirty diapers and moldy clothes. The kind of smells no one should ever be breathing in.

And though the house appeared abandoned, it wasn't empty.

With every step it became evident there was a human presence—someone still occupying a place time itself seemed to have forgotten. At first, we couldn't identify who it was.

That uncertainty disappeared the moment we met him. As we headed toward the firepit, we walked past an unscreened open window. As we stood between the house and the firepit, a head suddenly popped out a window, immediately startling us. We were met by a face of a man clouded in the smoke of his dangling cigarette. "Hold on, I'll be right out!"

My husband and I exchanged confused looks. "Who is that?", I asked. Shrugged shoulders met my gaze. "I have no idea", my husband whispered.

He emerged from the back of the house.

"Joey," he said, extending a filthy hand toward us. "I live here now."

Decay has a way of announcing itself before words are ever spoken. Long before authority is challenged, the environment tells the truth. Neglect leaves a signature. Disorder advertises itself. The Bible always talks about how fruit doesn't lie. You don't have to look hard to know when something has been left too long without oversight.

The discomfort was immediate. A thin sheen of cold sweat clung to his forehead, making his pallor even more pronounced. He wore no shirt. His movements were quick, erratic, and restless. A haze of cigarette smoke seemed to trail him from room to room. But what struck me most wasn't just his appearance—it was the way he spoke, the way he stood, the way he claimed the space as his own. This wasn't shelter to him.

It was territory.

Despite the overwhelming stench of sweat, grime, and stale smoke, we did our best to mask our reaction. I was still dealing with lingering effects of long COVID and couldn't detect the full force of the odor, but my husband's expression betrayed his unease. Joey's filthy nails and overall appearance made it clear he had been living in squalor for some time.

Yet he greeted us with an unsettling warmth—the kind that can hide deeper layers of instability.

"We pastor the church across the street," my husband said, shaking his hand. "And it looks like we're going to be buying this property."

Joey's response came quickly, almost casually, as though he had anticipated the conversation.

"Buying the property?" he muttered, thinking out loud. Then, without waiting for clarification, he finished his thought. "I don't see why. I've been here for a while now. I live here. I'm taking care of it."

In that moment, it became clear:
We thought the keys would be granting us access. Turns out someone had beat us to it and we were not the only claim being made on that house.

Time spent in a place does not equal authority over it. Survival gets mistaken for stewardship when accountability is absent. Proximity is not permission, and endurance does not confer ownership—no matter how confidently it's claimed.

Joey believed that time spent occupying the space had granted him authority. What he called care was survival. What he called ownership was proximity. And what he claimed as permission had never been his to give or receive.

Still, he stood firmly planted—unmoved by legality, unmoved by truth, unmoved by the reality that the house did not belong to him.

What we did not yet understand was this:
A squatter does not leave simply because they are confronted with truth. Those keys meant nothing to him. Apparently neither did the imposing plans of purchase.

This squatter had claimed his territory. We would be forced to enforce our authority.

Chapter Four

The House of Horrors

Joey's response to our intentions was blunt, as though the idea of his eviction had never crossed his mind. He was unapologetic—confident in his position as the "new owner" of the property. His certainty caught us off guard.

"Well, that may be the case at the moment," my husband said carefully, "but in a few days we're finalizing the purchase of the property, and you will no longer be able to stay here."

"That won't be happening," Joey replied, his voice firm and final. "I'm here now, and I'll be taking care of it."

Without waiting for a response, he turned and headed into the house. "Do you want to come inside so I can show you the work I've put in?" he added, as though this crumbling structure were a point of pride rather than a refuge of neglect.

My husband and I exchanged a quick glance before reluctantly following him inside. After all, we had come to see the property, but nothing could have prepared us for what awaited us.

As we stepped through the back kitchen door, the air immediately thickened. My senses—dulled for months during recovery from COVID—suddenly sharpened. The stench was overpowering. Sour. Nauseating. It clung to everything: the walls, the furniture, the very air we breathed. Flies buzzed aimlessly through the rooms, confirming what our instincts already knew—something was terribly wrong here.

We entered the house through the door Joey had exited upon greeting us; the kitchen. It was a devastating scene. In the center of that kitchen floor was a pile of trash, stacked high and scattered across the floor. But this wasn't simply clutter—it was chaotic accumulation. Clothing, books, shoes, diapers, forgotten items layered into a disturbing mound that had clearly been untouched for far too long. This mountain of refuse served as a visual record of prolonged neglect. It wasn't just a trash heap; it was a reflection of decay—of the house, of the lives that had passed through it, and of the spiritual condition of the one who now occupied it.

What struck me were the "memories" that were peeking through the trash. The academic certificate that was awarded to a child for being a good student was now neighbors to a dirty diaper and animal feces. I had to stop and wonder if these children had really lived in this filthy disgusting chaos or had this happened after they left? But even so, why leave behind an award that should have been displayed on a background and not discovered in a pile of trash? How had this environment become normal to its inhabitants? How?

Joey appeared unfazed. He gestured toward the pile casually. "Those are my work partners," he said, pointing to a broom and a snow shovel leaning against the wall. The shovel, dulled by grime, stood as a silent accomplice in a survival strategy that had nothing to do with restoration or healing.

With unsettling ease, Joey began explaining the history of the house and its previous occupants. After the patriarch of the family passed away, the remaining tenants fled, leaving their dogs behind. Joey had taken them in as part of his new reality. He described how the former occupants returned once a week to feed the animals, leaving behind dog feces and urine that had soaked into every surface. This wasn't a temporary mess—it was a lifestyle formed over time.

As we surveyed the scene, the extent of the damage became painfully clear. Copper pipes had been stripped from the walls. Both the stove and the refrigerator were gone. The floors were caked with grime. What had once been a functional home had been gutted, leaving behind only evidence of how quickly something entrusted to care can fall into ruin.

The most heartbreaking sight, however, was the children's toys scattered among the debris. A school project, partially visible beneath the trash, stopped me cold. Children had once lived here. They had grown up in this environment—without guidance, without protection, without anyone stepping in to intervene.

Joey, unfazed, pointed toward the brown steps leading to the attic. "Those steps aren't brown," he said as he muttered through an uncomfortable giggle. "They're white. That's just dog crap caked into the linoleum."

The matter-of-fact tone in his voice sent a chill through me. There was no shame. No awareness that this wasn't normal. This was his standard now. This was life as he understood it—and there was no indication he wanted anything different.

He went on to explain how he was "excited" about cleaning up the property, as though the act of tidying could somehow entitle him to claim ownership. His words hung heavy with entitlement.

"I'm living here now."

We stood in silence, absorbing the full weight of what we were witnessing. Joey's claim to the house wasn't merely legal confusion—it was something deeper. Just as he had taken up residence in a decaying structure, so too can destructive forces take up residence in a person's heart, mind, and spirit—often without the individual realizing how deeply entrenched they have become.

Scripture is clear that neglect does not remain neutral. The Word consistently warns that what is tolerated eventually takes up residence, and what goes unchecked begins to redefine what feels acceptable. Over time, disorder stops alarming us, deception settles in, and dysfunction starts to feel normal. This is how bondage tightens its grip—not through sudden collapse, but through prolonged exposure to what should have been confronted.

This wasn't just a house in disrepair.

It was a warning.

Chapter Five

The Resistance

The weight of this situation did not escape us. We continued to silently stand there as Joey continued to speak, his voice calm but unwavering. There was conviction in his words—a sense of ownership that bordered on the absurd. The house, with its ruined walls and layers of filth, was his now. And he wasn't leaving.

He spoke at length about the work he had done, the long hours spent monitoring the fire pit in the backyard, the effort he believed he had invested in "restoring" the house. There was pride in his voice, even as the reality around him told a very different story. What stood before us was not restoration, but decay. Not renewal, but survival masquerading as progress.

Joey explained that when he first arrived, the house had been unrecognizable. We tried our best to connect the dots of his rambling tale of comings and goings, but the story line was blurry at best. From what we could gather, he had lived there and left and then at some point, returned.

Over the last few weeks, he claimed, he had worked tirelessly to clear the floors and impose some sense of order on the chaos. Suddenly, the persistent smoke we had smelled for weeks made sense. Burning trash wasn't an improvement—it was an attempt to manage dysfunction, to cope with something that was already beyond repair. And although the absurdity of the situation was clear to us, to Joey, he saw things differently.

As he spoke, compassion rose in us. Beneath the bravado and entitlement stood a man desperate for help, trapped by forces far greater than he could comprehend. His posture was defensive, but his story betrayed deep pain.

Overwhelmed, I finally asked a simple question. "When was the last time you ate?" His answer was heartbreaking. He hadn't eaten in days.

When I asked about the last time he had showered, he admitted it had been weeks. His shoes were too small; his feet covered in open sores. The pain was evident—but so was his resignation. This had become his normal. A life that was slowly destroying him, yet one he seemed unable—or unwilling—to leave.

I was an investigator for several years in the judicial system. I have been privy to many a heartbreaking story and up this point, had experienced them from an outsider's perspective. After years of walking through life with individuals who have survived horrific things, it takes a lot to shake me. But Joey's story was not only devastating, but it was also heartbreaking in so many ways. As he shared, I fought to contain the tears that wanted to spill out of my soul. How does one human being endure this level of catastrophic trauma?

The Bible is honest about moments like this. Compassion and clarity are not opposites, but they are not the same thing. Scripture shows us that pity can move the heart while still leaving a person bound. Wanting freedom and being ready for it are not identical. Even sincere desperation does not automatically produce change—because deliverance requires more than tears; it requires surrender and follow-through. The danger is rooted in the fact that the longer you entertain "sin", the harder it is to break up with it. It's no longer just something you do. It becomes something you are.

We asked if he wanted help.

That was when Joey broke.

Tears filled his eyes as he poured out the history of his life—family suicides, parental violence, addiction, trauma layered upon trauma. He wanted change. He wanted freedom. He begged for help.

With urgency, we began putting a plan together. The three of us stood there, in real time, brainstorming a plan that we thought we could execute. We finally asked him if he would accept treatment.

"Absolutely," he said, his response immediate and desperate. "I've been waiting for a break like this."

Within moments, things were set in motion. We gathered clothes, hygiene supplies, first aid items—anything we could think of—and prepared to take him to a treatment center about an hour away. As we walked back toward the church office to get everything ready, the weight of the moment settled in. We believed we were witnessing divine intervention—a soul standing at the threshold of rescue.

I had made it to the office first while my husband stayed behind with him in the house. While Joey rummaged through the debris to try and collect the items he needed, I had made it to the office and now found myself looking through the windows of the house, watching him move around inside. I stood there, with tears running down my face, trying to catalogue and process the conversation I had just experienced and that's when I heard the Holy Spirit say to me, "pay attention to what's happening across the street."

"What?" I whispered back.

"Pay attention to what's happening across the street" he firmly repeated.

Literally, in an instant, the totality of this book was downloaded in my spirit. I could see the title clear as day: The Squatter's Rights. And in that moment, I knew, this was bigger than a shower, some food, and a trip to rehab. This revelation would set people free.

A Brief Glimpse of Hope

Within an hour, Joey was on his way to rehab. He had showered and eaten and we had treated the blisters and wounds on his feet. We loaded him in the car and headed to a local processing center and after a few phone calls, we had found a rehab program that would take him. It was almost 60 miles away. Without hesitation, we fueled up the car and headed out.

During the drive, he cried repeatedly, gratitude spilling out between sobs.

"I've never had strangers help me like this," he said over and over. "Thank you. Thank you."

For a brief moment, we believed the turning point had come. He was on the path to freedom. We imagined the testimony that would follow—the redemption story that would emerge from the ashes of his past. We arrived, walked him in, hugged him good-bye and drove away with excitement in our hearts. A brief encounter had turned into a rescue mission, and we felt beyond blessed for the encounter. What an amazing turn of events!

We had an hour drive home, and we spent the whole time reflecting on what had just occurred. We couldn't wait to see Joey again, healed, set free, and made whole. It had only been a few hours from that first handshake with Joey but what a remarkable afternoon it had been.

But the next morning, everything changed.

Chapter Six

The Return of the Squatter

The morning began quietly. Now, with the house empty, my husband was excited to get things in order so we could move forward with the purchase. As my husband approached the church office just after sunrise, something across the street caught his attention. A window that had been bare the day before was now covered with a blanket, draped loosely as a makeshift curtain.

The house had been locked the night before. It should be empty.

Joey had been driven to a treatment center more than fifty miles away. He had no phone. No vehicle. Nothing that would have made a return possible—or so we thought.

As my husband drew closer, his heart sank. He paused and whispered a prayer under his breath. *Please, Lord, don't let that be Joey.*

But it was.

He carefully approached the living room window and peered through a small opening in the blanket. There he was...lying on a mattress on the floor. Joey was passed out. An empty bottle of vodka rested beside him. A crack pipe lay across his chest. My husband's heart sank. Freedom had been handed to him. He said he had been waiting for people like us. He promised this time would be different.

It didn't make sense. Joey had left willingly. He had cried. He had thanked us. He had agreed to treatment. And yet, somehow, he was back—re-entrenched in the very place he had promised to leave.

When my husband later told me what he had seen, disbelief washed over me. How had Joey returned so quickly? How had he even gained access? The doors had been locked. We had the keys.

And yet, there he was.

The Bible never presents relapse or returns as accidental. Scripture makes it clear that what is expelled but not confronted will attempt to re-enter. As a matter of fact, it guarantees an attempt will be made to reinvade. Locking doors is not the same as addressing occupation. It simply is not enough. Authority can be established on paper and still go unenforced in practice. This is why freedom requires more than removal—it requires active not passive resistance.

After waiting a few hours, my husband knew he had to confront him. He entered the house again—this time not as someone offering help, but as someone standing firm.

"Joey," he said, his voice steady but heavy with sorrow. "What are you doing here? You said you wanted help. We took you to rehab. What are you doing back here?"

The man who responded was not the same one who had wept in the car the day before. The softness was gone. The tone had shifted. He wasn't the same.

Joey's demeanor had hardened. His eyes were sharp. His voice was cold.

"I've been thinking about it," he said flatly. "I'm not going anywhere. You're going to have to evict me."

In that moment, it was clear a line had been drawn.

Whatever had loosened its grip the day before had returned with force. The friendliness was gone. The gratitude had evaporated. In its place stood defiance—entitlement reinforced by something darker and far more stubborn.

As my husband stood there, absorbing the weight of those words, the Holy Spirit spoke quietly to my heart once again:

"Pay attention to what's happening across the street."

This was no longer just a physical confrontation. It was a spiritual one.

Joey's return wasn't about relapse alone—it was about resistance. The forces that had occupied his life were not willing to leave quietly. And just as he had forced his way back into the house, those same forces were asserting their claim once again. The days of polite knocking were over. They were determined to rip that door off the hinges!

The door had been locked.

Authority had been established.

But the occupation had not yet been confronted. In a matter of hours, a broken man had morphed into a defiant man. *One that made it clear, the only way I'm leaving here is if you force me out. Are you ready for a fight?*

Chapter Seven

The Survey

After the confrontation, it was clear Joey had no intention of leaving. The tone had changed. The decision was no longer his to make. My husband took a firmer stance, informing him that the church was moving forward with the purchase of the property. He warned Joey that the house would be demolished and urged him to vacate for his own safety.

Joey resisted. The excuses ensued. We weren't quite sure what to do. He wasn't budging nor were we.

Arrangements were made for a demolition team to assess the property. We wanted Joey gone before the walk-through. There was no room for ambiguity now—plans were moving forward, with or without his cooperation.

The Bible is clear that authority does not require agreement to function. Scripture shows again and again that when purpose is established, resistance does not halt the process. There comes a moment when responsibility must move forward, even if someone refuses to cooperate. Waiting indefinitely is not mercy but rather a sign of avoidance. This is why it is important to understand where your authority comes from because the enemy will not leave without a fight. Your God given purpose trumps the enemy's misaligned plans. Own that truth and let it guide you.

On the day of the inspection, the project manager met with me outside the house.

"I need to inspect the inside," he said. "I have to assess the basement."

"We can't go inside just yet," I replied. "There's a squatter refusing to leave."

He nodded, unfazed. "Then I'll review the blueprints. By the looks of the outside, I take it there's a crawl space. Gotta figure out the total layout of the house."

Curious, I asked why the blueprints mattered so much.

"We need to identify danger zones," he explained. "Without a proper layout, our equipment operators could fall into the basement. We have to know where the crawl spaces are, where the foundation is weak, and whether there were additions made over the years. Some of that I can tell from the outside—but not all of it. I have to understand where the structure has been compromised."

Then he asked a question that lingered far longer than he could have known:

"What are the plans for the property?"

It sounded simple, but it carried weight.

"We're turning it into a parking lot."

"Got it. Well, the final use determines everything," he continued. "If the goal is just to cover the area, we can push the debris into the basement and seal it with dirt. But if the land is going to support something heavy—like the parking lot you want—that's a different story."

Scripture consistently connects preparation to purpose. The Word makes it plain that what something is meant to support determines how it must be built. Serious weight requires intentional preparation. Pressure exposes what assumptions try to hide. Purpose has a way of forcing clarity.

He paused before continuing.

"The foundation has to be solid" he said, as he gestured with his hand. "If we fill it with junk, it will collapse under pressure. So instead, we gut it completely and fill the space with solid ground."

*Fill the space with **solid ground**. The phrase echoed in my ears.*

Debris fills space. Junk fills space. But neither can bear weight. If something is meant to endure pressure—meant to support purpose—it cannot be built on what is discarded, unstable, or compromised. Only solid material can form a foundation strong enough to hold what will come next.

The Bible leaves no room for compromised foundations. Scripture teaches that anything unable to bear weight must be removed before building can continue. Material that collapses under pressure cannot be repurposed. Only what is solid, tested, and deliberately placed can sustain what is coming. Deliverance reshapes the structure, not just the surface.

The project manager completed his walk-around, making notes and asking follow-up questions. I wasn't sure if Joey could see us or hear us, but one thing was clear: demolition was no longer a possibility—it was inevitable.

Joey would have to leave.

Not because he agreed. Not because he understood. But because the purpose of the property demanded it. We wouldn't be bullied into surrendering our plans. Willingly or voluntarily, one way or another, he was done.

The project manager explained that none of the existing debris could be reused. For a project of this nature, it wouldn't work.

"We'll remove everything," he said. "Then we'll bring in fresh fill. Strong fill. Compacted material brought in from the outside. If this land is going to hold weight, it can't be filled with what was torn down. It has to be rebuilt from the ground up."

Truer words had never been spoken.

Chapter Eight

The Key

U p to this point, everything had felt reactive. We were respond-ing—to Joey's presence, to his resistance, to the deterioration of the house. But the truth was simpler, and far more unsettling: this situation had never lacked authority.

What it lacked was enforcement.

We had not broken into the house. We had not trespassed. We had not taken something that wasn't ours to touch. The rightful owner had given permission. She had entrusted us with access. And the keys my husband found were not symbolic. They were unequivocally a literal confirmation of that authority.

Still, Joey remained.

He had no legal right to the house. He had no ownership. He had no permission from the true owner. What he did have was proximi-ty—and a belief that simply being there long enough had granted him entitlement.

That belief mattered.

Joey had been allowed to stay by someone who never had the authority to grant permission in the first place, but that person had let Joey in. Yet, in his mind, that was enough. Time spent occupying the space became proof of ownership. Survival was confused with stewardship. Presence was mistaken for permission.

And when the door was locked—when boundaries were finally put in place—he didn't interpret that as a warning.

He kicked the door in and came back. No regrets- no pauses- no nothing.

Kicked. It. In.

That moment forced a realization we hadn't fully grasped before: having the keys did not automatically restore order.

Here's the thing about boundaries...boundaries are not arbitrary rules; they are conclusions drawn from evidence. They are a collection of data points that tell a story. And in this case, the data was everywhere—trauma responses, addiction, filth, squalor, no running water, no electricity, trash piled high and called "normal." Destruction does not need interpretation. It announces itself. Chaos and dysfunction were screaming from every square inch of this dwelling. Ten gallons of pristine white paint could not erase it.

Scripture makes clear that outcomes reveal truth. Fruit tells the story whether it's acknowledged or not. He was trespassing, we were not.

We had every right to be there.
He had none.

And yet, he refused to leave.

That's when it became clear to me—truth alone doesn't always move what has settled in deeply. Some things don't leave just because they're confronted with facts. Authority has to be exercised, or it will be ignored.

Our plans could not move forward with him still inside. The purpose of the property outweighed his resistance. What he wanted no longer mattered and not because we were being cruel and didn't care about him or his outcome. Our purpose was clear. Something bigger was being built, and it required space he was unwilling to relinquish.

What had occurred with Joey was not about punishment.
It was about purpose.

And it was the moment I understood that what we were facing wasn't just physical—it was spiritual. Everything about what was going on was 100% spiritual and it was manifesting itself in the physical.

Because just as Joey refused to relinquish a house he did not own, the enemy behaves the same way. Permission, once given—even improperly—does not dissolve on its own. It has to be revoked. Boundaries must be enforced. Authority must be exercised.

The *key* had been in our hands all along.

We simply hadn't used it yet.

Chapter Nine

The Demolition

The day finally arrived...

demolition day.

Across the street, an eerie silence hung in the air. Once, laughter had echoed through that yard. Life had been lived there. Stories had unfolded there. But now, those memories were coming to an end. Soon, everything would be reduced to rubble.

My husband did a walk through. The demolition team conducted a walk through. We had to make sure our warning had been adhered to.

The house was empty. The time had come.

The roar of machinery filled the morning as engines revved, preparing to tear down what remained of a small piece of history. What looked like loss on the surface was, in reality, necessary. Still, the emotions were complicated. Excitement, sadness, and regret existed in the same space, refusing to separate neatly.

Slowly, the demolition excavator moved into position. Its long yellow arm stretched outward, steady and deliberate. As I sat across the street watching, time seemed to slow. When the first blow landed, I wasn't prepared for how quickly it happened. What had once appeared solid—enduring—collapsed with startling ease.

The house caved in on itself. Dust and debris filled the air. But it wasn't the sight that caught me off guard—it was the smell. Years of neglect, filth, and decay burst free all at once. The stench of rancid urine and animal waste drifted across the street in a wave that had been sealed inside for far too long.

I couldn't help but wonder if this was how it was always meant to end. Surely, the architect who designed the home nearly a century earlier had imagined something different. And yet, here we were—watching decades of memories reduced to a growing pile of debris. The bulldozer struck again and again, its movements rhythmic and unrelenting. The creaking of the wood, the breaking of the glass, all of it was incredibly unsettling. Inch by inch, the structure collapsed under its own weight.

Twenty-six minutes later—that's all it took. As the dust settled, the shadow of what had once been stood over the scene. Demolition was over.

A house that had stood for nearly a hundred years—weathering seasons, families, and decades of change—was gone in less than half an hour. Fine dust floated in the air, settling over what remained. Flies were released from their confinement. All that was left was a heap of debris—memories buried beneath dirt, water-soaked sheetrock, rusted nails, and broken glass.

As I continued to watch, the moment felt bittersweet. What marked a new beginning for the church signaled the end of an era for that home.

Reality settled in quietly.

From where I stood, I could see my husband across the street, watching from a different angle. I wondered what thoughts were occupying his mind, sensing they mirrored my own. What is neglected long enough eventually collapses. What was once entrusted to care had been left unattended, and the outcome—however painful—was inevitable.

In the weeks that followed, there was no drama—only steady, deliberate work. The bulldozer finished its job. The trucks came in. The debris was hauled away. Eventually, the gravel was poured. The drains were laid. The land was leveled. In a matter of weeks, the parking lot emerged and the house was just a bittersweet memory.

And Joey? He slipped out quietly during the night. No confrontation. No resistance. No final words. No one saw him leave—but he was never seen again around our property. The demolition took place without incident, uninterrupted and uncontested. The house came down as planned.

Nearly two years later, I saw him again—riding a bicycle on the other side of town. He looked much the same as he had the day we first met him. Disheveled. Worn. Still wandering. I remember wondering, not with judgment but with sorrow, what house he had chosen next. Where he had found shelter. And whether he had ever found freedom.

The debris was hauled away completely. Nothing was buried. Nothing was reused. Fresh fill was brought in—the right soil, proper drainage, compacted layer by layer. Gravel was laid. Boundaries were set. Everything was done with intention, ensuring the land could finally bear the weight of what was being built.

What had once been reduced to ashes was not ignored or covered over. It was removed and replaced.

What stood there afterward was not just a parking lot.

It was solid ground. We had stayed true to our cause and opposition aside; we had reached our goal. There would be life despite of the death that had fought to remain.

No matter what the squatter had planned, his perceived permission was misplaced and meant nothing in the face of authority. He insisted on occupying space he was being told he had to leave—but once we acted on the authority we had been given, everything changed.

We would prevail.

But then again, that was God's promise to us. We had been given the vision and the authority to move forward. And God, as He always had, honored our purpose. That property would live again.

"To give them a beautiful headdress instead of ashes,
the oil of gladness instead of mourning,
the garment of praise instead of a faint spirit;
that they may be called oaks of righteousness,
the planting of the Lord, that He may be glorified."
— Isaiah 61:3 (ESV)

Chapter Ten

SECTION 2: A GUIDED DEBRIEF

By the time you reached the end of this story, you may have felt something familiar stirring beneath the surface. Discomfort. Recognition. Resistance. Or perhaps clarity. That is not accidental.

Looking back, I am convinced the Holy Spirit did not rush those moments for a reason. Time felt suspended—not dramatically, but deliberately. I was not being prompted to fix anything or intervene. I was being invited to observe. What unfolded across the street from our church was not simply a property dispute or a human crisis. It was a spiritual reality playing out in the physical world, layer by layer, in real time.

I remember standing still—watching, listening, discerning. The instruction was simple and unmistakable: *Pay attention to what's happening across the street.* That directive forced intentionality. God was interpreting events as they unfolded, revealing patterns, parallels, and principles I could not have grasped had I rushed past them. The clarity

I feel now is no different than it was then. I knew I was being shown something far bigger than a house.

So much so that I documented it. You've seen the pictures throughout this book. I recorded the demolition. The house on the cover of this book is the actual house. What you have read is not a metaphor constructed in hindsight—it is a lived experience captured in real time.

Part One was written to be read without interruption. The story needed to stand on its own. Before interpretation comes observation. Before application comes awareness. Too often, we rush to spiritualize what we have not fully seen. This book resists that impulse on purpose.

Part Two exists for reflection.

The chapters that follow are not designed to correspond one-to-one with the chapters you have just read. Instead, they slow the story down and examine it in phases. Each Guided Debrief draws from portions of the narrative to reveal a specific pattern as it unfolded—sometimes across several chapters, sometimes beneath the surface of a single moment. The goal is not to reinterpret the story, but to help you see what was already present as it developed.

What you will encounter here is not speculation or sensationalism. It is a guided debrief—a deliberate slowing down to examine what was already present. This is where patterns are named. Where parallels are drawn. Where spiritual realities that often go unnoticed are gently but clearly revealed.

I want to be transparent: not everyone understands or subscribes to the reality of the supernatural. That is not my role to resolve. I am not here to convince you of anything. I am here to explain what already exists, as I witnessed it, from my vantage point. My husband shares from the lens of pastoral authority. I share from lived experience and discernment. Together, we offer perspective—not pressure.

What you do with what you see is up to you.

God desires deliverance for His children. That conviction undergirds every page that follows. But deliverance begins with awareness. Many believers are unaware of how the enemy gains access—through trauma, neglect, compromise, and unguarded doors. Even more are unaware of how long he remains once given permission.

This section is an invitation to pause and look again.

To notice what you may have missed.

To recognize where something foreign may have taken up residence in places meant to be protected. To help you identify the squatters.

As you move through Part Two, resist the urge to skim. Let the observations sit. Let the questions linger. Pay attention—not just to what happened across the street, but to what may be happening within your own walls.

Because once you see it, you cannot unsee it.

And that is where freedom begins.

Chapter Eleven

Guided Debrief I: When Absence Becomes Access

This first Guided Debrief draws from the earliest moments of the story, when nothing appeared overtly hostile and no resistance had yet emerged. What unfolds here is not about sudden collapse, but about slow disengagement. Before confrontation, before enforcement, and before defiance, there was something quieter at work—loss, withdrawal, and unattended responsibility. This section examines how access is often granted long before occupation is recognized, and how authority can remain intact yet functionally absent when it goes unused.

***

Kitchen

Guided Observation: How Access Is Granted

One of the most revealing details appears quietly:

"She did not even have keys to enter it herself."

The rightful owner of the property no longer had the keys. This element is not merely narrative context; it is diagnostic in nature.

Authority had not been revoked, but it had gone unused.

Biblically, this is not a sign of surrender—it is dormancy. Authority can exist and still remain inactive. It can be legally intact yet practically absent. When authority remains dormant long enough, occupation begins to feel legitimate to those who enter later. What once would have been recognized as intrusion slowly begins to resemble entitlement.

It initiates an involuntary cycle:

Proximity is mistaken for permission.
Survival is mistaken for stewardship.
Presence is mistaken for ownership.

Scripture reflects this principle in Jesus' parable of the minas. Before departing, the nobleman entrusted resources to his servants and instructed them:

"He called ten of his servants and gave them ten minas and said to them, 'Engage in business until I come.'" — Luke 19:13

The instruction was clear. What had been entrusted was not meant to be hidden, preserved in fear, or left untouched. It was meant to be exercised. The expectation was participation, not passivity. Authority had been delegated, and with delegation came responsibility.

Dormancy was never the design.

When something is entrusted but not exercised, the surrounding environment begins to shift. Influence expands in the absence of intentional governance. Over time, what was meant to be managed begins to manage the one who was assigned oversight.

And this is where the conversation moves from theological to practical.

When speaking with people who are wrestling with patterns they feel trapped in, I will sometimes ask them something very simple:

Who is in charge of who?

Is __________________ your boss?
Or are you the boss of __________________?

Insert the *fear.*
Insert the **habit**.
Insert the **anger**.
Insert the **relationship.**
Insert whatever has been quietly setting the terms in your life.

It sounds almost elementary when said out loud. In fact, it carries the same tone as a child in the middle of a disagreement shouting, "You're not the boss of me!"

But beneath that childish phrase is a profound truth.

Someone is governing something.
Something is setting the terms.
Something is determining what happens next.

The issue is not whether authority exists. The issue is who is exercising it.

Because when authority goes dormant, something else eventually begins making decisions.

This explains why the environment shifted before anyone reentered the house. The atmosphere had changed because governance had been absent. Not maliciously rejected. Not formally surrendered. Simply unused.

And unused authority does not remain neutral for long.

What is most striking about this chapter is not the suddenness of decay, but its predictability.

The house did not fall into ruin because of a single event. It deteriorated through a sequence:

- Loss produced withdrawal

- Withdrawal produced absence

- Absence created vulnerability

- Vulnerability invited misuse

Each tenant arrived with intention, but without ownership. Temporary solutions replaced long-term stewardship. Over time, the condition of the house reflected not its original design, but the instability of those passing through it.

Scripture consistently shows that environments mirror governance. When authority is unclear, disorder is not far behind. Decline does not require malice—it only requires neglect.

In Proverbs 24:30–34, Solomon describes walking past a neglected field:

"I passed by the field of a sluggard,
by the vineyard of a man lacking sense,
and behold, it was all overgrown with thorns;
the ground was covered with nettles,
and its stone wall was broken down.
Then I saw and considered it;
I looked and received instruction.

A little sleep, a little slumber,
a little folding of the hands to rest,
and poverty will come upon you like a robber,
and want like an armed man."

The field did not collapse overnight. No enemy stormed it and no dramatic act of destruction took place. The wall broke down because it was left *unattended*. The thorns grew because they were not removed. A little neglect, repeated over time, produced visible ruin.

The same pattern unfolded in the house across the street. The decline was not immediate. It was incremental. And what was left unguarded slowly became ungoverned.

Guided Interpretation: Dormant Authority

One of the most revealing details appears quietly:

"She did not even have keys to enter it herself."

This is not merely narrative context; it is diagnostic in nature.

Authority had not been revoked, but it had gone unused.

Biblically, this is not a sign of surrender—it is dormancy. Authority can exist and still remain inactive. It can be legally intact yet practically absent. When authority remains dormant long enough, occupation begins to feel legitimate to those who enter later. What once would have been recognized as intrusion slowly begins to resemble entitlement.

It initiates an involuntary cycle:

Proximity is mistaken for permission.
Survival is mistaken for stewardship.
Presence is mistaken for ownership.

Scripture reflects this principle in Jesus' parable of the minas. Before departing, the nobleman entrusted resources to his servants and instructed them:

"He called ten of his servants and gave them ten minas and said to them, 'Engage in business until I come.'" — Luke 19:13

The instruction was clear. What had been entrusted was not meant to be hidden, preserved in fear, or left untouched. It was meant to be exercised. The expectation was participation, not passivity. Authority had been delegated, and with delegation came responsibility.

Dormancy was never the design.

When something is entrusted but not exercised, the surrounding environment begins to shift. Influence expands in the absence of intentional governance. Over time, what was meant to be managed begins to manage the one who was assigned oversight.

And this is where the question becomes practical.

When speaking with people who are wrestling with patterns they feel trapped in, I will sometimes ask them something very simple:

Who is in charge of who?

Is the addiction your boss?
Or are you the boss of your addiction?

It sounds almost elementary when said out loud. In fact, it carries the same tone as a child in the middle of a disagreement shouting, "You're not the boss of me!"

But beneath that childish phrase is a profound truth.

Someone is governing something.

Something is setting the terms.

Something is determining what happens next.

The issue is not whether authority exists. The issue is who is exercising it.

Because when authority goes dormant, something else eventually begins making decisions.

This explains why the environment shifted before anyone reentered the house. The atmosphere had changed because governance had been absent. Not maliciously rejected. Not formally surrendered. Simply unused.

And unused authority does not remain neutral for long.

Personal Items mixed in with debris

Guided Awareness: Identity Left Behind

The discovery of personal documents—birth certificates, Social Security cards, photographs, children's drawings—is not incidental.

These items represent identity, lineage, and belonging.

Scripture repeatedly connects identity loss with vulnerability. When identity is abandoned, disorder follows. What remained inside the house was not simply trash, but fragments of unclaimed stories—evidence of lives disrupted and responsibility displaced.

This was not just a neglected property. It was a space where identity had been left unguarded.

Looking Ahead

This chapter establishes a critical truth:

Permission does not automatically enforce authority.
Access does not prevent occupation.

What follows will reveal that once occupation takes root—even illegitimately—it rarely yields simply because truth is present. Confrontation alone does not remove a squatter. Authority must be exercised.

That reality emerges next.

Prayer for Awareness and Restoration

Heavenly Father,
Bring clarity where loss has blurred vision and pain has caused withdrawal. Reveal areas in my life where authority remains intact but unused. Show me spaces I have stepped away from out of grief, exhaustion, or avoidance.

Restore awareness without condemnation. Reestablish boundaries where responsibility has faded. Where identity has been neglected, bring truth. Where disorder has normalized, bring light.

Teach me the difference between absence and surrender, between permission and stewardship. I choose to reengage with what You have entrusted to me—not in fear, but in wisdom.

In Jesus' name,
Amen.

Chapter Twelve

Guided Debrief II: When Access Becomes Occupation

This section steps back from the narrative to examine the underlying pattern revealed in the chapter. The purpose is not to reinterpret the story, but to identify how authority, access, and neglect interact over time—often quietly and without resistance.

As you read, resist the urge to spiritualize prematurely. Instead, observe the progression. Pay attention to where responsibility shifts, how boundaries weaken, and what fills the space when rightful authority remains present but disengaged. This is not about assigning blame. It is about recognizing patterns that repeat in homes, families, churches, and individual lives.

***

Upstairs Bedroom (1)

Guided Observation: When Damage Becomes Visible

What unfolded in that house is not unique. It is simply easier to recognize when the damage is physical. When destruction is visible, decay is harder to deny. What follows is not theory, but pastoral interpretation—an explanation of how false ownership takes root when trauma opens the door and rightful authority is left unexercised.

It could be stated that the overarching spiritual story taking place in this house is an everyday occurrence in the lives of many Christians. This is exactly what happens in our spiritual lives when we allow the enemy to take residence. Jesus warns in John 10:10, *"The thief comes only to steal, kill, and destroy."* That is his mission—not only to ruin us, but to spread that ruin to those around us.

In this story, trauma stole the owner's joy and hope. It killed the desire to stay and heal. As a result, the promise of what this home could have been was abandoned by those who could not walk through the healing process and was subsequently destroyed by those who defaced and degraded it.

Over time, this house became a stronghold for abandonment, addiction, alcoholism, and darkness. And just as the lives residing inside decayed, so did the house itself. The paint peeled. The roof and gutters crumbled. The once-manicured lawn became overgrown. Trash and broken furniture filled the yard. What was once full of potential became a picture of neglect and destruction.

Upstairs Bedroom (2)

Guided Interpretation: How Access Becomes Occupation

Scripture warns us in 1 Peter 5:8, *"Be sober, be vigilant; because your adversary the devil, as a roaring lion, walketh about, seeking whom he may devour."* The enemy is always looking for an opportunity to strike, and trauma is one of his easiest entry points. In this story, tragedy became leverage. What began as grief was exploited, turning a place of love into a place of ruin. This had nothing to do with the rightful owner of the home not wanting to heal. Quite the contrary—she felt that healing would come if she just did not address the memories tied to the home. However, avoidance is not healing. Instead, it can become the golden ticket the enemy is waiting for to move into that unhealed place and wreak havoc.

This is what happens when the enemy is not only given access but allowed to stay. If he is not removed, destruction continues—unchecked and unchallenged. And the consequences are never isolated. Just as the decay of that house affected the entire neighborhood—bringing mess, chaos, and stench—a life overtaken by darkness spreads pain to everyone nearby.

Guided Awareness: Reclaiming What Was Left Unattended

The question becomes personal: ***Have I opened a door and left it unattended?***
Just as a house can be restored, so can a life—but restoration requires action. The enemy must be evicted. The damage must be addressed. And the rightful Owner—Jesus—must be invited back into the space.

Scripture reminds us in 2 Corinthians 5:17, *"Therefore, if anyone is in Christ, he is a new creation. The old has passed away; behold, the new has come."* When Christ moves in, He does not simply clean up what is broken. He makes all things new.

For those who feel stirred, convicted, or ready to take that step, a prayer of surrender and restoration is provided at the conclusion of this Guided Debrief.

A Prayer for Those Ready to Reclaim What Was Lost

If, as you've worked through this Guided Debrief, you've recognized places in your own life where doors were opened and left unattended—places marked by trauma, loss, or long-standing patterns—you may feel ready to respond. This prayer is not offered as obligation or pressure, but as invitation. Take a moment. Read slowly. And if the words reflect the posture of your heart, make them your own.

A Prayer of Surrender and Hope in Jesus

Lord Jesus,

I come before You with nothing left—empty, broken, and weary. I have searched for answers in so many places, but none have satisfied my soul. My heart is heavy, my spirit crushed, and I don't know where else to turn. But in this darkness, I call upon Your name.

Jesus, today I confess that I believe You are the way, the truth, and the life, and I need You now more than ever. I have tried to carry my burdens alone, and they are too heavy for me. I lay them at Your feet. I surrender my pain, my doubts, my fears, and all the things that have led me to this moment.

I don't have the strength to fix myself, but I believe You can. I don't know what the future holds, but I trust that You hold my future. Please, Lord, step into my life. Fill this emptiness with Your presence. Take my brokenness and make something new. Forgive me for the times I have run from You. Today, I run to You.

Be my refuge, my healer, and my Savior. I don't have all the answers, but I choose to believe that You are the answer. Hold me close, Lord. Let me feel Your love. Give me the strength to take one more step—to hold on just a little longer—knowing that You are with me.

Thank You for hearing me, for loving me, and for never giving up on me. I give You my life, my pain, my everything.

In Jesus' name,
Amen.

Chapter Thirteen

Guided Debrief III: When the House Is Left Empty

This debrief examines one of the most sobering moments in the story: help was offered, hope surfaced, and a plan was put in place—yet bondage still returned. That tension matters. It forces us to separate what feels like breakthrough from what Scripture calls transformation. What follows is not a judgment of a man in crisis, but a clear-eyed look at a pattern the Bible repeatedly exposes: when freedom is initiated but the "house" remains unfilled and unguarded, occupation does not stay gone. This section is designed to help you recognize why temporary relief can happen without lasting change—and what must be different for deliverance to hold.

***

Guided Observation: What We Witnessed

When individuals do not receive deliverance from what has them bound, they still leave doors open to Satan. It becomes a spiritual "legal right," so to speak.

We caught a glimpse into Joey's heart when we heard his cries for change. His tears were real. His desperation was genuine. His request for help was sincere. However, saying we need a change—no matter how emotional the moment—is very different from doing what is scripturally necessary to walk in lasting freedom.

Deliverance is hard. It is costly. It requires discipline. And when someone truly repents from a lifestyle, repentance means to turn away from it entirely.

Guided Interpretation: Why It Did Not Hold

Joey wanted change, but he was not willing to fully submit his life to Christ. That unwillingness left the door open for the enemy to return.

In the parable of the strongman (Matthew 12:43–45; Luke 11:21–26), Jesus teaches that a demon may be cast out of a house, but if the house is left empty—unfilled by the presence and authority of Christ—the spirit will return. And it does not return alone. It brings seven others stronger than itself.

In Luke's account, Jesus first establishes the framework of authority:

"When a strong man, fully armed, guards his own palace, his goods are safe; but when one stronger than he attacks him and overcomes him, he takes away his armor in which he trusted and divides his spoil" (Luke 11:21–22, ESV).

Authority protects what it governs. But when greater authority intervenes, control shifts.

Jesus then continues:

"When the unclean spirit has gone out of a person, it passes through waterless places seeking rest, but finds none. Then it says, 'I will return to my house from which I came.' And when it comes, it finds the house empty, swept, and put in order. Then it goes and brings with it seven other spirits more evil than itself, and they enter and dwell there, and the last state of that person is worse than the first" (Matthew 12:43–45, ESV; cf. Luke 11:24–26).

The warning is not about disorder—it is about vacancy. A house may appear clean. It may appear orderly. But if it remains unoccupied by rightful authority, it is vulnerable to reoccupation. Deliverance removes. Ownership fills. Authority secures.

This explains what we witnessed.

Although we prayed with Joey, exercised authority, and helped remove him from immediate danger, he did not follow through with true repentance. His emotions were intense, but his submission was incomplete.

Satan was not threatened by temporary relief. As long as Joey remained spiritually unguarded, the enemy retained access. Authority was challenged briefly—but never enforced long-term.

This was not failure of compassion.
It was a failure of surrender.

Guided Awareness: What This Reveals

This pattern is not unique to Joey.

When deliverance is pursued without repentance, doors reopen. When repentance is delayed the inevitable happens; strongholds remain. And when the house is not filled, occupation returns—often worse than before.

This requires a different strategy.

Emotional moments can open the door to change, but only sustained obedience closes it. People can get lost in the moment and fall victim to their own emotional rollercoaster. The desperate prayer, "God, if you get me out of this, I promise that..." only to find that "thing" showing back up again and being embraced in our arms. Death bed prayers are not enough.

True freedom is not achieved by desperation alone; it is secured through submission, discipline, and the continual filling of one's life with Christ.

The question is not whether help was offered.
The question is whether authority was embraced.

***

A Prayer for True Deliverance and Surrender.

Lord Jesus,

I come before You with honesty and humility. I recognize that emotional moments alone cannot sustain freedom. Search my heart and reveal any areas where I have desired relief without surrender, change without obedience, or deliverance without repentance.

Where doors have been left open, show me how to close them fully. Where I have resisted discipline, teach me to walk in truth. Fill every empty place in my life with Your presence so that nothing unholy may return.

I renounce every agreement made with darkness—knowingly or unknowingly—and submit myself fully to Your authority. I do not want temporary relief; I want lasting transformation.

Strengthen me to walk this out daily, not just emotionally, but obediently.

In Jesus' name,

Amen.

Chapter Fourteen

Guided Debrief IV: When Authority Is Challenged

This debrief examines what happens after truth has been established but before order is restored. Permission had been granted. Access was legitimate. Ownership was clear. And yet, occupation continued. What unfolds here reveals a critical spiritual distinction: knowing the truth does not automatically enforce authority. When unlawful occupation is confronted, resistance often intensifies—not because authority is unclear, but because it is finally being applied. This section is not about conflict; it is about clarity, resolve, and the moment when enforcement becomes unavoidable.

***

Guided Observation: When Resistance Reappears

What stands out immediately in this phase of the story is not simply Joey's return, but **how** he returned.

The house had been locked and access had been restricted. On a positive note, Joey had willingly left and verbally agreed to treatment.

Every outward indicator suggested that the situation had been resolved. And yet, he came back. His return was not marked by confusion or repentance—it was assertion. He reentered the space, reclaimed physical ground, and positioned himself as immovable. His language was no longer grateful or desperate. It was firm, defiant, and confrontational.

"You're going to have to evict me." This shift matters.

What appeared the day before as openness and willingness to change was replaced by resistance and intimidation. The goal was no longer help—it was control. This was not merely relapse. It was **intentional reoccupation**.

Resistance does not appear randomly. It often surfaces precisely when authority is no longer ambiguous.

Guided Interpretation: Intimidation and the Limits of Passive Authority

Scripture consistently shows that intimidation is a primary tactic when illegitimate claims are challenged. Second Timothy 1:7 reminds us that fear does not originate with God. Fear is used to unsettle, delay, and pressure those standing in truth to reconsider their position.

Throughout Scripture, intimidation precedes retreat—or enforcement. Goliath relied on threats long before he ever advanced. His power depended on hesitation. David's victory came not from ignoring the threat, but from refusing to submit to it.

The same dynamic was at work here.

Joey's words carried no legal authority, yet they were delivered with confidence. His goal was not negotiation—it was testing resolve. When he declared that eviction would be required, he was probing whether authority would retreat under pressure.

This reveals a sobering truth: **authority that is not exercised is treated as optional by those who benefit from disorder**.

Up to this point, everything had felt reactive. We were responding—to decay, resistance, and disruption. But the situation had never lacked authority.

What it lacked was enforcement.

Truth had been present from the beginning. Permission had been granted by the rightful owner. We had the keys. Eventually, the deed would confirm what was already true. Joey knew this. And still, he resisted. Why? Why was he so dead set on staying?

Because truth alone informs. However, truth means nothing if authority fails to act.

Scripture warns, "My people are destroyed for lack of knowledge" (Hosea 4:6)—not because truth is unavailable, but because it often remains unused. Knowledge without action leaves authority dormant. And dormant authority invites continued challenge.

Guided Awareness: The Line Between Clarity and Enforcement

This is where the case study becomes personal because many believers live informed but unenforced lives—aware of truth, yet hesitant to act on it. Boundaries are understood but not maintained. Authority is possessed but not exercised. That gap matters.

Just as Joey refused to relinquish a house he did not own, the enemy behaves the same way. Permission—once granted, even improperly—does not dissolve on its own. It must be revoked. Boundaries must be enforced. Authority must be exercised.

Resistance does not always indicate failure. Often, it confirms that authority has finally been applied correctly.

This is not about aggression. It is about resolve.

Retreat is not humility when God has already made authority clear. It is surrendering ground that was never meant to be forfeited. Something larger was being built—and it required space that resistance was unwilling to surrender.

A Prayer for Courage to Enforce God-Given Authority

Heavenly Father,

Thank You for truth, and for the authority You entrust to Your children.

Where I have known what is right but hesitated to act, give me clarity and courage. Teach me the difference between understanding authority and exercising it.

Show me where boundaries must be enforced—not out of fear or anger, but obedience. Where permission was granted improperly, help me revoke it. Where resistance has gone unchecked, help me stand firm.

I choose clarity over confusion, obedience over hesitation, and purpose over passivity.

I will not surrender ground that does not belong to the enemy.

In Jesus' name,
Amen.

Guided Debrief V: Removal, Replacement, and Solid Ground

This final debrief examines what happens when authority is no longer delayed, negotiated, or explained—but exercised. By this point in the story, truth has been established, resistance has surfaced, and enforcement has become unavoidable. What follows is not symbolic. It is decisive. Scripture is clear that deliverance does not end with exposure or confrontation. Freedom is secured through removal, replacement, and the establishment of something strong enough to bear weight. This section addresses what must happen after occupation ends, and why restoration requires more than clearing space—it requires building on solid ground.

***

Demolition Day

Guided Observation: Removal Is Not the Same as Resolution

The demolition of the house was not dramatic—it was deliberate.

What stood for decades came down in minutes. Walls collapsed. Rooflines caved. Hidden damage was exposed. What had been sealed inside—filth, decay, contamination—was released into the open air.

The smell alone told the truth: this structure could not be repaired. It had to be removed.

Scripture consistently affirms this principle. There are moments when restoration is not achieved through repair, but through removal.

Jesus teaches in Matthew 7:24–27 that foundations matter. A house built on sand cannot withstand pressure. No amount of surface improvement can compensate for compromised ground. When collapse comes, it reveals what was already unstable beneath the surface.

This is why partial measures fail.

Covering debris does not strengthen a foundation.
Burying dysfunction does not produce stability.
Removing visible disorder without addressing what lies beneath guarantees collapse under pressure.

The house had to come down—not because it lacked history, but because it could no longer support purpose.

Guided Interpretation: Replacement Is Required for Lasting Freedom

Scripture is explicit that deliverance requires replacement.

Jesus warns in Matthew 12:43–45 that when an unclean spirit leaves a house and finds it empty, it returns—bringing others stronger than itself. The issue is not removal alone; it is vacancy. An empty space invites reoccupation.

This principle applies both spiritually and structurally.

The debris from the house was not reused.

Nothing was buried.

Nothing was repurposed.

Fresh fill was brought in from the outside—strong material, compacted layer by layer, engineered to support weight. This was not cosmetic improvement. It was foundational replacement.

Second Corinthians 5:17 declares, *"If anyone is in Christ, he is a new creation. The old has passed away; behold, the new has come."* Scripture does not describe salvation as renovation. It describes it as transformation.

Likewise, Romans 12:2 commands renewal—not adjustment. Replacement requires intention. It requires discipline. It requires obedience.

Deliverance that is not followed by filling will not hold. Freedom that is not reinforced by truth, obedience, and sustained authority will collapse under pressure.

Guided Awareness: Solid Ground Bears Weight

The purpose of the land determined the process.

If the goal had been temporary use, debris could have been buried. But the land was being prepared to bear weight—vehicles, movement, ongoing use. That required solid ground.

Scripture makes the same distinction spiritually.

Ephesians 6:10–18 outlines the believer's posture not as reaction, but preparation. Truth, righteousness, peace, faith, salvation, the Word of God, and prayer are not defensive accessories—they are structural reinforcements. They establish stability where pressure is expected.

James 1:22 reminds us to be doers of the Word, not hearers only. Knowledge informs. Obedience stabilizes.

This is the difference between relief and freedom.

Relief removes discomfort.
Freedom establishes order.

What God builds, He builds to last.

The question this final chapter asks is not whether something has been removed—but whether something strong enough has been put in its place.

Guided Conclusion: Authority Restored

The house did not fall because it was attacked. The decision was made to dismantle it. It was no longer a place of safety. It was death. We understood the decision that needed to be made, and the house could not remain. The house came down because it had been compromised too long to remain standing. Neglect did that.

It was our decision to bring purpose back to that parcel of land. We did not replace it with emptiness. We replaced chaos, catastrophe and emptiness with solid ground.

Isaiah 61:3 declares that God gives *"a beautiful headdress instead of ashes, the oil of gladness instead of mourning, the garment of praise instead of a faint spirit—that they may be called oaks of righteousness, the planting of the Lord, that He may be glorified."*

Oaks do not grow in unstable soil.

What God restores, He stabilizes. What He delivers, He reinforces. What He removes, He replaces.

Authority was exercised.
Occupation ended.
Purpose moved forward.

***

A Prayer for Complete Restoration and Enduring Freedom

Heavenly Father,

I thank You for the authority You have given through Jesus Christ. I acknowledge that freedom is not sustained by exposure alone, but by obedience, replacement, and truth lived out daily.

Where You have removed what did not belong, establish what does. Where disorder once occupied space, build righteousness. Where instability existed, lay solid ground.

I choose not just deliverance, but endurance.

Not just relief, but restoration.
Not just freedom for a moment, but authority that lasts.

Plant me where I can bear weight.
Strengthen what You have reclaimed.
And let what You build in me bring You glory.

In Jesus' name,
Amen.

Chapter Sixteen

SECTION 3: FOUNDATIONS FOR FREEDOM

How Entry Happens: Mind, Body, and Soul

Before we talk about deliverance, we must first understand **how entry happens**.

Scripture teaches us that the human person is made up of **three distinct yet connected parts: mind, body, and soul**.

"May your whole spirit, soul, and body be kept blameless..." — *1 Thessalonians 5:23*

This matters because **access does not happen in only one way**.

Just as a house has more than one window or door, the human person has **multiple points of entry**. When any one of these areas is left unguarded, access can be gained—often slowly, quietly, and without immediate awareness.

The Mind

The mind is where thoughts, beliefs, memories, and interpretations live.

Intrusion in the mind often begins with:

- Lies that feel logical

- Repeated negative thoughts

- Distorted beliefs about self, God, or others

- Trauma memories that replay without resolution

Scripture reminds us that battles often begin here:

"As a man thinks in his heart, so is he." — *Proverbs 23:7*
"Be transformed by the renewing of your mind." — *Romans 12:2*

When false beliefs go unchallenged, they become **agreements**. And agreements create **access**.

The Body

The body stores experiences, especially pain and trauma.

Intrusion through the body can happen through:

- Chronic stress

- Trauma responses

- Addictive behaviors

- Physical coping mechanisms meant to numb or survive

Even when the mind forgets, the body remembers. This is why some reactions feel automatic or out of proportion—they were learned in moments of survival.

The Apostle Paul acknowledged the body as a sacred dwelling:

"Do you not know that your body is a temple of the Holy Spirit?" — *1 Corinthians 6:19*

When the body is treated as expendable or disconnected from the soul, **boundaries often weaken**.

The Soul

The soul is the seat of emotions, will, identity, and desire.

Intrusion in the soul often looks like:

- Deep emotional wounds

- Unresolved grief

- Shame

- Fear

- Hopelessness or despair

The psalmist speaks directly to the condition of the soul:

"Why, my soul, are you downcast?" — *Psalm 42:5*

When pain in the soul goes unattended, it creates **spaces where things settle that were never meant to stay**.

What a Boundary Is (and What It Is Not)

A **boundary** is a God-given line that protects what is sacred.

A boundary says:

"This is where I end and you begin."

"This is what I allow and what I do not."

"This is how close something may come to my heart."

Boundaries are not walls but rather they serve as gates that create a line of demarcation that says, "this is as far as you go".
Healthy boundaries do not isolate you. On the contrary, they **protect** you.   .

This bears repeating because if you have been surrounded by people that have pushed past your boundaries, the very mention of this topic may already be causing great distress. Boundaries are not walls meant to shut people out; they are lines of protection that preserve what is sacred. They allow connection without compromise and relationship without loss of self. When boundaries are healthy, they do not cut you off from others—they keep you **anchored in truth, safety, and clarity**.

Boundaries are also not meant to make you feel guilty. Guilt often enters when someone pressures you to abandon the very line that is keeping you safe. This can sound spiritual. It can sound relational. It can even sound loving. But when a boundary is violated, the body and spirit often respond before the mind catches up.

You may feel it in your gut.
A tightening.
A heaviness.
A quiet warning that something is off.

That internal signal is not rebellion. That internal signal is called **discernment**. And discernment is a powerful asset in the vault of wisdom.

Scripture affirms this kind of wisdom:

"The prudent see danger and take refuge, but the simple keep going and pay the penalty." — *Proverbs 22:3*

Healthy boundaries do not mean you are unkind, unforgiving, or unloving. They mean you are attentive. They mean you are guarding what God has entrusted to you. Even Jesus did not entrust Himself to everyone, though He loved fully and freely.

When someone consistently challenges your boundaries, dismisses them, or spiritualizes their removal, it is worth pausing to ask why. Protection is often mistaken for distance by those who benefit from your access.

Boundaries are not about control. But they are most definitely about **stewardship**.

And when a boundary is honored, peace follows. When it is violated, unrest often takes its place. Learning to recognize that distinction is part of restoring order to the house.

What a boundary is:

- A form of stewardship

- An act of wisdom

- A way of guarding the heart (Proverbs 4:23)

- A tool for maintaining peace, safety, and alignment with truth

What a boundary is not:

- Rejection

- Unloving behavior

- Punishment

- Control

- A lack of forgiveness

Boundaries are not about keeping people out. They are about protecting what God has placed within you. When boundaries erode, access expands and lines become blurry. And when those lines blur, access expands unchecked—and intrusion eventually follows.

Walking you through these explanations are not about blame. They are designed to bring about awareness.

Small Entrances, Big Consequences

Return again to the image of the house.

The **white picket fence** marks the boundary.
The **yard** is the space that surrounds your inner life.
The **sidewalk** is the path of access.
The **porch** is familiarity without intimacy.
The **front door** is full entry.

And then finally...inside the house—the ***couch*** **sitting nicely in your living room.**

The couch represents **rest, comfort, authority, and permanence**. It is where you sit. Where you settle. Where you live from.

At first, nothing feels dangerous. You don't invite an intruder into your house—you invite a **guest**. Guests are familiar. Guests are welcomed. Guests come inside and spend time with us in the living room.

And where do guests usually sit?

On the couch.

When someone sits on your couch, they are no longer outside your boundaries. ***They are inside your space.*** Conversations happen there. Influence is exchanged there. Time is shared there. Vulnerability is trusted there.

This is how access becomes normalized. Think of it as a grooming process. Little by little, idea by idea, nudge by nudge, access is gained.

What began as a visit starts to last longer than expected. What was meant to be temporary begins to feel familiar. And familiarity lowers discernment. The guest becomes comfortable. But more importantly, with your guard down, the guest presents no threat.

Just like Joey. He started off as a guest. He ended up as a squatter.

The Squatter

In legal terms, a **squatter** is a person who occupies or uses property **without the legal right, permission, or consent of the owner**.

There is no title.
No lease.
No authority.

A squatter's presence is unlawful, even if they appear settled or act as though they belong. Often, squatters do not enter by force. They take advantage of what is **vacant, unattended, or neglected**.

Time does not equal permission.
Presence does not equal ownership.
Comfort does not equal authority.

Joey was never meant to live there. He was not the owner. But once access was granted and authority was left unexercised, the guest stopped acting like a guest. Over time, he became a **squatter**—claiming space, creating disorder, and refusing to leave.

The enemy does not arrive announcing destruction. He comes as a visitor. He sits. He stays. And when he is not confronted, he settles in.

Very few intrusions begin at the front door.
And almost none announce their intention to take the couch.

Most begin quietly—at the fence.

Example One: A Small Entrance

A recurring sense of discomfort shows up in a relationship, a conversation, or a situation. Nothing feels openly harmful. Nothing seems worth addressing. So you stay at the fence—engaging, explaining, minimizing what you feel.

Over time, the discomfort becomes familiar. The gate opens. The influence moves into the yard.

The couch is not taken yet—but peace begins to erode.

Example Two: A Moderate Entrance

During a season of stress or grief, a coping habit develops. It brings relief. It helps you get through the day.

What began as survival becomes routine.

The influence comes inside and stays long enough to pull up a chair. Decisions begin to bend around it. Life adjusts to accommodate it.

Rest is shared now.
Authority is no longer fully yours.

Example Three: A Significant Entrance

A deeply painful experience goes unprocessed. The door is not intentionally opened—but it is left unattended.

Shame enters quietly.
Fear makes itself at home.
Hopelessness takes a seat.

Eventually, the couch is occupied.

This is the goal of the intruder—not just access, but **residence**.

The Common Thread

What lingers long enough seeks comfort.
What becomes comfortable seeks control.
And what controls the couch begins to shape how the house functions.

If you recall the images earlier in this book—the trash, the destruction, the chaos—that devastation did not happen overnight. Once the couch was taken, order collapsed. And without awareness, the house became unrecognizable. But what do you do once you realize living in bondage is no longer an option?

Why Deliverance Is Necessary

Nearly thirty years ago, I lived in a large Victorian-style home. The original structure had the expected features of its era, but an addition had been built onto the back of the house years before we moved in. Unlike the rest of the home, which used older accordion-style water heaters, this addition had floor heaters mounted along the wall.

One winter, we began to notice a smell.

At first, it was faint—easy to dismiss. But with each passing day, it grew stronger. Eventually, it became impossible to ignore. What we were smelling was decay.

I remember walking from room to room, trying to locate the source. I sniffed walls, corners, vents—until we narrowed it down to the bonus room in the back of the house, the addition. I got on my hands and knees, following the smell until it led me directly to one place: the heater along the wall.

We took a flashlight and looked inside.

The culprit was a dead mouse, stuck to the heating coils.

The problem was not identifying what was wrong. The problem was what it would take to remove it.

That addition had been built years earlier, and there was no guarantee that prying off the heater cover wouldn't break the unit entirely. If it broke, we weren't looking at a simple repair—we were looking at hundreds, possibly thousands of dollars in damage. Money we did not have.

So we made a hard decision.

We left the mouse where it was and hoped it would dry out.

It eventually did—but the consequences lingered far longer than we expected.

For nearly two years, that smell would return every winter. The moment the heater kicked on, the stench filled the room. What had once been a place we enjoyed became a space we avoided. We stopped spending time there. We adjusted our lives around the problem rather than dealing with it directly.

The mouse was no longer alive—but its presence still dictated how we lived.

This is what happens when something that does not belong is left in place because removal feels too costly.

The issue is not always a lack of awareness.
Sometimes it is the fear of what it will take to address the problem.

But decay does not resolve itself simply because it is inconvenient to remove. It continues to affect the atmosphere of the house.

This is where deliverance becomes unavoidable.

Deliverance is **intentional**. It is the willingness to confront what has settled in, even when removal feels disruptive, uncomfortable, or costly. It is the decision to stop organizing life around an intruder and instead restore the space to what it was meant to be.

Without deliverance, we may survive—but we will not fully rest. Without deliverance, we may function—but peace will remain compromised. Sure, we didn't have to move out of our house due to a dead mouse in the heater unit. It was more of an inconvenience than an outright catastrophe. But I wonder what I would have done if there had been four or five mice stuck to that coil. Would I have been as willing to live with that level of stench, or would I have taken the risk to pull that cover off and neutralize the problem?

Deliverance is not dramatic. Deliverance is an intentional decision to take *"off the cover"*. Deliverance is deliberate. Awareness alone is not enough.

Recognizing that something does not belong is an essential first step—but recognition does not remove what has taken up residence. Once I realized the mouse was the source of the problem, awareness alone didn't make the stench disappear. I remember thinking, "how did it get in there in the first place?" For me, it was two-fold; seal the entrance and eliminate the smell. Sealing the entrance was easy and less costly. Neutralizing the smell wasn't.

Likewise, in the case of deliverance, knowing how access happened does not automatically restore order. Therefore, understanding ownership does not, by itself, reclaim authority that has gone unexercised.

This is why **deliverance is necessary**.

Deliverance is required when something remains in the house that no longer has the right to be there—but continues to influence how the house functions. It becomes necessary when access has turned into occupation, and occupation has disrupted peace, clarity, identity, or rest.

Scripture makes this distinction clear.

Jesus did not only teach truth—He **removed what opposed it**.

"The Spirit of the Lord is upon Me... He has sent Me to proclaim freedom for the captives and release from darkness." — *Luke 4:18*

Deliverance is not about fear or spectacle. In reality, it is about **alignment**. It is the process of removing what entered unlawfully so that what is rightful can be restored.

Without deliverance:

- The couch remains occupied.

- Rest remains compromised.

- Authority remains contested.

- And in my case, the smell acting as disorder continued to affect the entire house.

This is why simply "coping" is not enough. This is why insight alone does not always bring freedom. And this is why some patterns persist even after understanding has grown.

Deliverance is not the first step—but it is a **necessary one**.

It follows awareness.
It follows ownership.
And it requires willingness.

Until unlawful occupants are removed, restoration remains incomplete.

The good news is this: deliverance does not require striving, strength, or spiritual performance. It requires **rightful authority**—and that authority begins with ownership, which will be addressed in the chapters that follow.

Reflection

Take a moment to sit with these questions honestly and without judgment:

1. What is happening in my life right now that feels out of place?

2. What feels like an intruder—something that doesn't belong but has become familiar?

3. Where might I be lingering at the fence instead of guarding it?

4. What have I normalized that once felt uncomfortable or wrong?

5. Which area of my "house" feels least peaceful right now?

Please understand that awareness is not condemnation. It is a gift and is the beginning of freedom.

A Pastoral Prayer

Father God,

I come before You with honesty and humility.

You know every room of my heart—every space I've guarded and every place I've left unprotected.

If there is anything in my life that does not belong, bring it into the light with gentleness and truth.

Show me where access has been given without my realizing it.

Restore my discernment. Strengthen my boundaries and heal what has been wounded.

If I have never fully surrendered ownership of my life to You, I do so now.

I acknowledge Jesus Christ as Lord and Savior.

I invite You to take rightful ownership of this house—my heart, my mind, my soul.

Where there has been confusion, bring clarity.

Where there has been intrusion, bring order.

Where there has been fear, bring peace.

Teach me to guard what is sacred,

to walk in wisdom,

and to live in the freedom You intend for me.

In Jesus' name,

Amen.

Chapter Seventeen

Salvation: Who Owns the House?

The Question Is Not Who Has the Keys

When we ask, *"Who owns the house?"* we are not asking who can come and go.

Not who has access. Not who has keys. But who holds the ***deed***.

Access can be shared. Keys can be handed out. Locks can be changed.

Why is the deed so important?

In real estate, a **deed** is the legal document that establishes ownership. It identifies who has the lawful right to possess, control, protect, and enforce authority over a property. The deed—not the keys—determines who has standing.

Remember Joey?

At some point he may have had keys to the house and yet he still had no legal right to live there. Joey moved freely in and out and still was not the owner. Joey even acted as if the house belonged to him, but without the deed, it was just that, *an act.* He had absolutely no authority whatsoever.

<u>Ownership is established by the deed.</u>

This distinction matters spiritually. This is where many people confuse **access** with **ownership**. They allow influences into their lives, hand out keys, tolerate presence, and assume familiarity equals permission. But access alone does not grant authority.

<u>Salvation is the moment the deed is transferred.</u>

Scripture makes this clear:

"You are not your own; you were bought at a price." — *1 Corinthians 6:19–20*

That price was paid through the death and resurrection of Jesus Christ. Salvation is not symbolic. It is **transactional**. Ownership changes hands.

Keys Are Not the Same as Ownership

There is a strong possibility that at some point you have seen a key or two that have stamped on them *DO NOT DUPLICATE.* Yet that warning does not stop people from duplicating them. You've probably done it a time or two. And that's the point, the warning on the key is not enough.

We all know this; keys can be borrowed. Keys can be stolen. Keys can even be copied without permission.

Therefore, possessing a key does not mean someone owns the house. It only means they have **access**.

This is why keys are not the issue. And this is why ownership must be enforced.

Even when a deed is properly filed and ownership is clear, a squatter can still move in. They may occupy space they have no right to be in. This behavior goes on to disrupt the function of the home, and mistakenly conveys the message that somehow, they belong. Their presence does not invalidate the deed—but it does require **intervention**.

In the physical world, when a squatter refuses to leave, the owner does not negotiate. The owner exercises authority. Law enforcement is called. Sometimes the court gets involved. Specific eviction language is used. Orders are issued. Authority is enforced.

The squatter is removed—not because they agree to leave, but because they never had the right to stay. The same principle applies spiritually.

Salvation establishes ownership.
Deliverance enforces it.

Permission, Authority, and Resistance

This distinction is not theoretical—we lived it.

When we encountered resistance in that house, my husband had the **keys**—and more importantly, he had **permission from the rightful deed holder** to be there. He was not trespassing. He was acting under authority derived from ownership, even though he himself was not the owner.

Joey did not have that.

Joey had no keys that were legitimately given.
Joey had no permission from the deed holder.
Joey had no legal standing.

And yet, despite that, he remained unphased and we encountered resistance.
He did not simply leave when confronted. He demanded that we enforce our right of eviction. His.

Resistance did not mean Joey belonged there. It meant authority had to be **enforced**.

This matters spiritually.

Jesus, the Keys, and the Deed

Scripture tells us that Jesus holds the keys:

"I hold the keys of death and Hades." — *Revelation 1:18*

But this is where many believers become confused.

Jesus did not take the keys to leave His people powerless. He took the keys to **transfer authority**.

"I have given you authority..." — *Luke 10:19*

Yes—Jesus gave us the keys.

But the keys do not function independently of ownership.

Keys grant **access**.
The deed establishes **authority**.

The keys only work **in conjunction with the deed**.

This is where Christians often get tripped up. They know they have been given authority, but they have never settled the question of ownership. They attempt to use keys without understanding what gives them standing.

In legal terms, someone may have keys to a property—but if they are not acting on behalf of the owner, their authority can be challenged.

Spiritually, Jesus does not hand over keys apart from ownership.
He gives authority to those who **belong to Him**.

"But to all who did receive him, who believed in his name, he gave the right to become children of God." — John 1:12 (ESV)

Ownership, Authority, and Enforcement

Spiritually, Jesus does not hand over keys apart from ownership.
He gives authority to those who belong to Him.

Salvation is not symbolic. It is not emotional agreement or intellectual alignment. It is a transfer of ownership from one kingdom to another. Scripture describes salvation as a *decisive act in which jurisdiction changes hands.*

Colossians 1:13–14 (ESV)

"He has delivered us from the domain of darkness and transferred us to the kingdom of his beloved Son, in whom we have redemption, the forgiveness of sins."

This passage is explicit. Salvation is not partial rescue or temporary access. It is deliverance *from* one domain and transfer *into* another. Redemption establishes rightful ownership. Forgiveness confirms the transaction. The deed is secured because Christ has paid the price.

Salvation establishes the deed.

But ownership alone does not remove every challenge. Scripture shows that authority must be exercised for what has been secured to function as intended.

Jesus makes this clear when He speaks of keys—not as symbols, but as instruments of governance.

Matthew 16:18–19 (ESV)

"And I tell you, you are Peter, and on this rock I will build my church, and the gates of hell shall not prevail against it. I will give you the keys of the kingdom of heaven, and whatever you bind on earth shall be bound in heaven, and whatever you loose on earth shall be loosed in heaven."

Keys are given only after identity is established. Authority follows belonging. Binding and loosing are not passive ideas; they require action. Keys that remain unused do not unlock doors. Authority that is not exercised remains dormant.

Authority activates the keys.

Still, Scripture is honest about one final reality: illegal occupation does not vacate simply because ownership exists or authority is acknowledged. Enforcement is required.

Jesus explains this principle through the parable of the strong man.

Luke 11:21–22 (ESV)

"When a strong man, fully armed, guards his own palace, his goods are safe; but when one stronger than he attacks him and overcomes him, he takes away his armor in which he trusted and divides his spoil."

The strong man's confidence is rooted in unchallenged occupation. Basically, he's the spiritual squatter. His authority is assumed because no one has confronted it. Removal occurs only when greater authority is exercised decisively. This passage does not describe confusion—it describes enforcement.

It is important to remember that deliverance does not question ownership.
It enforces what ownership has already secured.

Salvation establishes the deed. Authority activates the keys. Deliverance enforces what ownership has already secured.

This is not a progression of intensity—it is a progression of clarity. Each step builds upon the last, and none function properly in isolation. Ownership without authority leaves access unresolved. Authority without enforcement leaves occupation intact. Scripture does not separate what God intends to work together.

Resistance does not mean authority is absent. However, it does mean authority must be **asserted**.

Why Language Matters

In the physical world, authority is exercised through **language**. Orders are spoken. Declarations are made. Legal standing is asserted verbally and formally.

The same is true spiritually.

Scripture reminds us:

"Death and life are in the power of the tongue." — *Proverbs 18:21*

Deliverance is not emotional force. It is not striving nor is it spiritual performance. Deliverance is the rightful use of **language that aligns with ownership**.

Until authority is spoken, intrusion often remains. And in this case, the squatter stays. The reality is that until language aligns with the deed, unlawful occupants continue to act as though they belong.

Salvation Comes First

This is why salvation must precede deliverance.

Without salvation:

- authority is unclear

- resistance feels confusing

- freedom is temporary

Jesus Himself warned about a house that was cleaned but left unoccupied:

"When an unclean spirit goes out... it finds the house empty, swept, and put in order." — *Matthew 12:43–44*

Order without ownership is vulnerable.

Salvation ensures the house is not just clean—but **inhabited by the rightful Owner**.

Reflection

Take a moment to consider these questions honestly:

1. Who holds the deed to my house?

2. Who has keys—and how did they get them?

3. Am I trying to exercise authority without first settling ownership?

4. Have I mistaken resistance for lack of authority rather than a call to enforce it?

These are not questions of condemnation but rather are designed to guide you to a place of clarity. It is our prayer that by now you've already experienced those moments of clarity where you have literally heard the bell go off and seen the light come on and things finally make sense. If so, may this prayer help clean up the blurry lines and bring you the clarity that you've been seeking.

***

A Pastoral Prayer of Salvation and Surrender

Father God,

I come before You with honesty and humility.

I acknowledge that I cannot govern my life on my own.

I believe that Jesus Christ is the Son of God,

that He died and rose again,

and that He alone has the authority to save and restore.

I surrender ownership of my life to You.

I place the deed of this house in Your hands.

I invite You to take Your rightful place—

to sit on the couch,

to establish peace,

and to restore order.

Where there has been confusion, bring clarity.

Where there has been resistance, bring resolve.

Where there has been unlawful occupation, prepare the way for removal.

I trust You with what belongs to You—

my heart, my mind, my soul.

In Jesus' name,

Amen.

Chapter Eighteen

Deliverance: Enforcing What Ownership Secured

Once ownership has been established, something else becomes necessary.

Authority must be exercised. The only reason we keep repeating this is because understanding deliverance is rooted in grasping the concept of authority.

Deliverance is not about discovering who owns the house—that question has already been settled. Deliverance is the enforcement of what ownership secured. It is the moment authority moves from belief into action, from understanding into declaration.

In both legal and spiritual terms, ownership without enforcement leaves space for continued intrusion. Authority must be asserted. And authority is exercised through **language**.

This is why deliverance is not silent. And it is not accidental. It is intentional, spoken, and ordered.

What follows is not about volume or performance, but about alignment—speaking from a place of settled ownership and delegated authority.

Authority, Emotion, and the Way Jesus Modeled Deliverance

It's important to talk honestly about volume.

In many deliverance settings, voices rise. People cry. Some shout. Others tremble. Emotions surface—sometimes unexpectedly. This is not automatically wrong. Deliverance touches places that have often been silent for a long time. When freedom begins to break through, the body and emotions frequently respond.

Deliverance is not sterile. It is not detached. And it is certainly not unemotional.

But it also cannot be run by emotion alone.

Emotion may accompany deliverance, but it must never replace authority. Volume may increase, but it does not create power. Intensity does not equal effectiveness. Authority does not come from how loud something is spoken—it comes from **who stands behind what is spoken**.

This is where Jesus becomes our clearest guide. Why? Because Jesus IS the AUTHORITY.

Jesus never relied on theatrics to cast out demons. He did not perform for the crowd or escalate emotion to gain control of a situation. His authority was not something He worked up—it was something He simply carried.

At times, His words were remarkably brief.

"Jesus rebuked the unclean spirit, saying, 'Be silent, and come out of him!'"
— *Mark 1:25*

That was it.

There was no prolonged exchange. There was no need for raised voices and there was no dramatic display. The truth of the moment was powerful enough to stand on its own.

Authority did not need embellishment.

At other times, His words were firm and unmistakable, spoken into moments that were already emotionally charged.

"Come out of the man, you unclean spirit!"
— *Mark 5:8*

This encounter took place in a deeply unsettling setting. The man lived among the tombs. He was isolated, tormented, and visibly distressed. The atmosphere was chaotic. Yet Jesus did not mirror the chaos. He did not absorb the emotion of the moment or amplify it. He spoke into it with clarity and command.

In another moment, deliverance occurred in a synagogue.

"Just then a man in their synagogue who was possessed by an impure spirit cried out, 'What do you want with us, Jesus of Nazareth? Have you come to destroy us?'"
— *Mark 1:23-24*

This man was not outside the worshiping community. He was in a sacred space. And when Jesus' presence confronted what did not belong, the reaction was loud and public. But he didn't respond to it without restraint. Instead, Jesus' response was measured.

"'Be quiet!' said Jesus sternly. 'Come out of him!'"
— *Mark 1:25*

The man convulsed and cried out—but the spirit left.

What was happening in that moment was not harm, nor an escalation of pain. Jesus was not inflicting suffering or provoking chaos. He was exposing and confronting what had taken up residence where it did not belong.

To darkness, authority feels like torment—not because it is cruel, but because it signals removal.

The House Revisited

This is where the image of the house matters again.

When we first walked through that home, the chaos was undeniable. Debris covered the floors. Trash was piled in corners. The stench hung in the air. What should have been livable space had become unrecognizable—not because it was meant to be that way, but because something unlawful had been allowed to remain.

The house itself wasn't evil. It wasn't in the walls or hidden in the floors. As chaotic as the entire dwelling had become, the structure wasn't the problem. The damage came from **occupation**.

And when occupation is confronted, it reacts. The power of light is unmistakable.

Just as that house revealed its condition the moment light entered—when doors were opened, when rooms were exposed—so too does unlawful spiritual occupation respond when authority shows up. The reaction can be loud. It can feel disruptive. It can look uncomfortable.

But the noise is not the cause of the problem.
It is the *evidence* of it.

The smell did not mean the house was beyond repair. The debris did not mean restoration was impossible. The chaos did not mean ownership was lost.

It meant something that did not belong had been living there.

This is what we see in Scripture. When Jesus entered synagogues, homes, streets, and graveyards, His presence exposed what had been hidden. And when exposure happens, reaction follows. It's the third rule of the basic laws of physics; for every action, there is an equal and opposite reaction. And Jesus was not one to step back from a situation where he stood in complete authority.

Jesus never recoiled at the reaction let alone mistake resistance for failure. And He never confused noise with power.

That was not His *modus operandi*.

Jesus was succinct in his movements. He addressed the source when he spoke with authority and as a result that decision restored order. That is what deliverance does.

It restores order.

For far too long, individuals—Christians included—have been sweeping mounds of debris, trash, chaos, and dysfunction under the rug of "religion." The flies are still there. The stench is still there. The giant rug of dysfunction is still there.

That is not deliverance. That is denial. Deliverance confronts the enemy head-on so the house can breathe again.

Filling the Space

Remember the pre-demolition survey conversation, when the project manager paused and asked me what we planned to build there?

He explained that once the structure was removed, the space could not simply be left as it was. It couldn't be filled with debris or temporary material. And it certainly couldn't be ignored. Whatever replaced what had been removed would need to **bear weight**. If the ground wasn't repaired properly, whatever was built on top of it would eventually fail.

Later, I watched the demolition take place. I watched as the debris was hauled away. But more importantly, I also watched what came after.

That plot of land did not stay empty.

I saw trucks bring in rock and filler—layer after layer—meant to stabilize what had once been compromised. I watched heavy rollers press everything down, compacting the ground so it wouldn't shift under pressure. I saw the leveling take place, the careful grading, the drains installed so water would move where it was supposed to go instead of pooling beneath the surface.

Nothing about that process was rushed.
Nothing about it was casual.

The land had to be **repaired**, not just cleared.

Only then could it move into the next season of its life—something functional, stable, and able to serve a purpose. In this case, a parking lot. A space meant to support weight, traffic, and movement without collapsing under strain.

This matters when we talk about deliverance.

When something unlawful is removed from a life, the space it occupied cannot be left hollow or hastily filled. Jesus warned us about houses that are swept clean but left empty—not because freedom is dangerous, but because emptiness is vulnerable.

Deliverance creates space. But restoration determines whether that space holds.

You cannot replace chaos with nothing. You cannot rebuild on unstable ground. And you cannot expect lasting freedom without intentional repair.

The places where intrusion once existed must be filled deliberately—with truth, with identity, with Christ's presence. The ground has to be stabilized. Compacted. Leveled. Drainage addressed. Old weaknesses repaired.

Freedom that lasts is not just about what was removed.
It's about what was **rebuilt**.

And rebuilding takes intention.

A Prayer of Deliverance and Sealing

(Fill-in-the-Blank)

Father God,
I come before You in humility and confidence, knowing that ownership of my life has already been settled through Jesus Christ.

I acknowledge that Jesus is Lord over my life—
over my mind, my body, my soul, and every space within this house.

In the name of Jesus,
I now exercise the authority that has been given to me as a child of God.

I specifically bring before You the area(s) where I am seeking deliverance:

____

(name the fear, pattern, lie, addiction, oppression, trauma, mindset, or influence)

I renounce every agreement—known or unknown—that gave access to what does not belong to You.
I withdraw permission for this influence to operate in my life.

In the authority of Jesus Christ, I **bind** every spirit, influence, and assignment connected to
____ and I command it to leave now.

You have no legal right here.
You have no authority in this house.
You must go in Jesus' name.

I declare that this space belongs to Jesus Christ alone.

Now, Father, I ask that You **fill every space** that has been cleared.

I loose truth where there were lies.
I loose peace where there was unrest.
I loose clarity where there was confusion.
I loose healing where there was brokenness.
I loose freedom where there was bondage.

Holy Spirit, I ask you to seal this work—guarding my mind, stabilizing my heart, and strengthening my boundaries.

I declare that this house will not remain empty.
It is filled with Your presence.
It is governed by Your truth.
It is protected by Your authority.

I commit to rebuilding on solid ground—
to renewing my mind,

to guarding what You have restored,
and to walking in alignment with You.

I thank You that deliverance is not partial, temporary, or fragile.
What You remove, You replace.
What You restore, You sustain.

I receive the joy, peace, and freedom that follow obedience.

In the mighty and authoritative name of Jesus Christ,
Amen.

Chapter Nineteen

Closing Chapter

If you've made it this far, take a breath.
A long one.

What you've read is weighty—not because it was dramatic, but because it was honest. This story was never meant to overwhelm you. It was meant to slow you down long enough to notice what often goes unnamed. To help you recognize patterns that rarely announce themselves, but leave evidence everywhere once you know how to look.

What happened across the street from our church was not complicated, but it was layered.

Authority existed long before it was exercised.
Access was granted long before it was questioned.
Resistance only appeared once boundaries were enforced.
And removal did not occur until clarity replaced hesitation.

That pattern is not unique to a house. It's a snapshot of what can happen when individuals allow the enemy space in their house.

If at any point while reading you felt discomfort, hesitation, or an internal nudge you couldn't quite explain, pay attention to that. Conviction does not always arrive loudly. Sometimes it comes as recognition. Sometimes as relief. Sometimes as the quiet realization that something you've tolerated has been asking to be named.

This is not about fear. It has always been about awareness. Awareness is a gift.

Awareness is not meant to paralyze you.
It is meant to position you—on *SOLID GROUND*.

One Final Question: Who Owns the House?

Everything you've read points to a simple truth: **occupation only ends when rightful ownership is restored—and enforced.**

That applies to property.
It applies to land.
And it applies to lives.

Some of you may have picked up this book out of curiosity. Maybe you were interested in the supernatural. Maybe you thought you were reading a strange true story. Instead, you encountered something far more personal.

Scripture teaches that every person was created for relationship with God. When that relationship is broken, other things begin to occupy space—fear, shame, control, addiction, despair, self-reliance. Rarely all at once. Usually over time.

Jesus Christ came to restore what was lost.

Salvation is not about religion or having everything figured out. It is about **restored ownership**. It is the decision to acknowledge that something else has been governing space in your life—and to invite Christ to take His rightful place, not as a guest, but as Lord.

You do not need certainty to take that step.
You do not need confidence.
You only need willingness.

If something stirred in you while reading—recognition, longing, clarity—this is your invitation to respond.

A Prayer of Surrender and Restoration

Jesus,
I acknowledge that I need You.

I recognize there have been places in my life left unguarded. Spaces filled with things that brought harm instead of peace. I believe You are the Son of God, that You gave Your life to restore what was broken, and that You offer new life through grace.

Today, I surrender what I can no longer carry.
I invite You to take Your rightful place.

Forgive me, restore me, and make me new.
I trust You with what comes next.

In Jesus' name,
Amen.

A Moment of Final Reflection

Before you close this book, consider this honestly:

- If something felt familiar, what was it?

- If resistance rose, what boundary might be near?

- If clarity surfaced, what truth has been waiting to be acted on?

You are not responsible for everything at once.
But you are responsible for what you now see.

"If anyone, then, knows the good they ought to do and doesn't do it, it is sin for them." — James 4:17

A Gut Check Worth Listening To

This is not a diagnostic list.
We pray that you see it as an invitation to discernment.

As you reflect, notice if any of these resonated:

- You recognized patterns that were once normal to you

- Access may have been granted through grief, exhaustion, or avoidance

- You've known the truth for a long time but delayed acting on it

- Boundaries felt clear in theory but difficult to enforce

- Resistance increased when you tried to bring order

- You confused endurance with faithfulness

- You hoped time would resolve what obedience required

If even one of these stood out, it does not mean you failed. It means you are becoming aware. And awareness is where restoration begins.

A Final Word: Do It Afraid

Courage does not require certainty.
Obedience does not wait for comfort.

If you are waiting to feel fearless before you act, you may wait longer than necessary. Scripture never promises that obedience will feel safe. It promises that it will be supported.

You may feel unsure.
You may feel inexperienced.
You may feel afraid.

Do it anyway.

Set the boundary. Get the deed in order. Use the keys. And act on what has already been established.

Jesus has already gone before you.

Fear does not disqualify obedience.
Often, it confirms it.

Closing Prayer

Heavenly Father,
Thank You for what You have revealed and for the clarity You provide through truth. Where fear has delayed obedience, give me courage. Where clarity has been present but unused, strengthen my resolve.

Help me to act with wisdom and humility. I choose not to remain passive where You have given authority. I choose obedience—even if the next step is taken afraid.

Establish solid ground beneath my feet.
Remove what does not belong.
Replace it with what can endure.

I trust You with what comes next.
In Jesus' name,
Amen.

Chapter Twenty

Continue the Journey

Crowned **Warrior Leadership Institute** is designed primarily to equip and support ministry leaders as they navigate emotional health, trauma, spiritual authority, and restoration. It also serves as a central place to connect with us, access additional resources, and continue the conversations introduced in this book. If you are seeking guidance, clarification, or a next step—whether for personal growth or ministry leadership—you are welcome to begin that journey here. To learn more or get in contact with us, visit **Crowned Warrior Leadership Institute** by scanning the QR code below.

Scan for more information

About the authors

Dr. Giovanna "Giovy" Sanders is a ministry leader, author, and speaker with a heart for helping people recognize, confront, and restore areas of life that have been compromised over time. With a background in leadership, ministry, and emotional health, she brings clarity to complex spiritual realities through storytelling, discernment, and lived experience.

Her doctoral studies opened the door for in-depth research into the effects of trauma and how it manifests in the lives of Christians—how believers cope, how they endure, and how unresolved trauma often becomes entangled with spiritual language, including the pursuit of deliverance. Through her research, Giovy observed a recurring gap: many believers were seeking freedom but lacked a practical, grounded framework to understand what they were experiencing or how healing, authority, and deliverance intersect.

When the Holy Spirit revealed this book to her, it became clear that God desired a practical and accessible way to help those bound by trauma and in need of deliverance—one that addressed real questions people often carry but are too afraid to ask. This book was written to bring understanding where there has been confusion, permission where there has been silence, and clarity where fear has kept people stuck.

Giovy writes from the place where theology meets real life, guiding readers toward awareness, restoration, and intentional obedience rooted in truth rather than fear.

Bishop Dennis Sanders is an ordained minister and seasoned pastor with decades of experience in shepherding individuals and communities through spiritual growth, restoration, and accountability. His pastoral insight is shaped not only by biblical training and ministry leadership, but also by personal experience.

More than thirty years ago, Dennis walked through his own deliverance from drugs and alcohol. That journey informs the way he approaches ministry today—rooted in Scripture, exercised with humility, and grounded in the understanding that freedom is both spiritual and practical. He speaks from the perspective of one who has been restored, bringing clarity to the realities of deliverance, authority, and sustained transformation.

Dennis contributes to this book through guided debriefs and theological reflection, helping readers understand how spiritual principles operate in real-world situations. His voice anchors the narrative with wisdom, compassion, and lived credibility.

Together, Giovy and Dennis serve in ministry as senior pastors, walking alongside others as they learn to recognize rightful ownership, exercise authority responsibly, and rebuild on solid ground.